ENDURING
A CRISIS
— OF —
FAITH

RICO MARANTO

D1600291

ENDURING
A CRISIS
— OF —
FAITH

RICO MARANTO

CFI

An imprint of Cedar Fort, Inc.
Springville, Utah

ISBN 13: 978-1-4621-4473-0

Published by CFI, an imprint of Cedar Fort, Inc.
2373 W. 700 S., Suite 100, Springville, UT 84663
Distributed by Cedar Fort, Inc., www.cedarfort.com

Library of Congress Control Number: 2022949778

Cover design by Shawnda T. Craig
Cover design © 2023 Cedar Fort, Inc.
Edited and typeset by Liz Kazandzhy

Printed in the United States of America

10 9 8 7 6 5 4 3 2 1

Printed on acid-free paper

I dedicate this book to my dear wife, Elizabeth.
Her continuous support and encouragement
enabled me to endure my crisis of
faith and write this book.

Other Books by Rico Maranto

Servant Leadership in Action:
How You Can Achieve Great Relationships and Results
(Contributing Author)

Sadie the Sad Striped Snake: The Value of Inclusion

Terry the Trustworthy Tarantula

CONTENTS

Acknowledgments

I wish to express my sincere gratitude to everyone who gave of their time and talents to improve this book or shared their stories so we could view crises of faith through various lenses. I am especially grateful for April Gustafson Phillips, David Ostler, Elizabeth Maranto, Jamie Turner, Jeff Honeycutt, Joshua Kosmicki, Judy Maranto, and Sammy Maranto. Their feedback, insights, and assistance were invaluable.

INTRODUCTION

*"Seeds of faith are always within us; sometimes it takes
a crisis to nourish and encourage their growth."*

—Susan L. Taylor[1]

Let me begin by sharing an account from a man named Steven Farrell.

In early 2018, I was an active, believing Mormon—serving in a wonderful, small ward as a second counselor in the bishopric. It was at this time that I discovered troubling aspects of Church history (a long story in itself). Through a process of extensive research, I entered stage 4 faith and was thrown into my faith crisis, and down the rabbit hole I went.

The dark and despairing feelings are hard to express. I felt alone, isolated, and deeply depressed. My trust in the Church and its leaders diminished instantly.

"Who can I talk to about this?" I frequently asked myself.

My relationship with God was fractured. How could He have misled me about these truths for so long?

---

1. Susan L. Taylor Quotes, "Seeds of faith," AZ Quotes, accessed Nov. 9, 2022, https://www.azquotes.com/quote/522701.

I was in deep anguish over my lost faith and my egocentric identity as a choice and elite member of God's one true church on the earth. Even worse, I was scared I might lose more than my faith: my family, my community, or even my marriage.

My faith crisis lasted for months and even now it hangs around and reminds me of what I lost.

When I shared my concerns with my bishop and stake presidency, there was no one who understood or would anguish with me. There was no inspiration, only condemnation. I was warned to stop my pursuit of finding truths about Church history and was told that if I didn't, I would join the ranks of apostates. Even those closest to me, people I love deeply, compared me to Judas Iscariot and Korihor. I was even told that I was possessed by an evil spirit, my home was full of darkness, and my future was bleak.

I (sometimes) knew better, though. How can I blame them for these harsh words? I knew the people closest to me are only expressing what they have been taught—that these words are coming from fear and not from love. I continue to hold onto that belief during each time my faith crisis returns.[2]

This account is representative of the crises of faith many Latter-day Saints experience. This book is written for all who experience a crisis of faith and for those who love and support them. My hope is that those who read this book will understand: (a) the divine purpose of a crisis of faith, (b) strategies for enduring a crisis of faith, and (c) how to help others who are experiencing a crisis of faith.

This book will apply to everyone because every spiritual journey is similar, but it will also not fully apply to anyone in particular because every spiritual journey is different. In this book, we will explore five stages of faith as a template for spiritual development, though I also acknowledge it is impossible to produce a template that universally fits

2. Courtney Farrell, "Every member needs to read this book," review of *Bridges: Ministering to Those Who Question*, by David B. Ostler, Amazon, Sept. 21, 2019, https://www.amazon.com/gp/customer-reviews/R3VD6K8FJK2P38/.

every person's unique spiritual experience. My hope is that those who read this book will identify parallel experiences in their own lives and discover concepts they can apply "that it might be for [their] profit and learning" (1 Nephi 19:23).

My intent in writing this book is not to resolve specific concerns that cause us to doubt our faith. This book will not answer questions about Church history, doctrine, culture, practices, or policies, though I mention many of these throughout the book to provide context. Instead, my intent is to reframe doubt and crises of faith so we can better understand their divinely designed purpose and develop the mindset, tool set, and skill set to "endure [them] well" (Doctrine and Covenants 121:8).

In this book, we will discuss faith, the stages of faith, crises of faith that occur at various stages in our spiritual development, and how crises commonly stem from unfulfilled needs. We will discuss in detail what the mystic St. John of the Cross called "the dark night of the soul,"[3] the most severe crisis of faith. We will also explore strategies for enduring crises of faith and for helping others endure them.

Crises of faith are important developmental experiences in our spiritual journeys.

Crises of faith are important developmental experiences in our spiritual journeys. As such, many faithful people will experience a crisis of faith. David B. Ostler, a former bishop, stake president, mission president, and author of *Bridges: Ministering to Those Who Question*, conducted a 2018 survey of leaders in The Church of Jesus Christ of Latter-day Saints that revealed that 97% had a friend or family member who had experienced a crisis of faith. Another survey he conducted of Latter-day Saints who were experiencing a crisis

---

3. St. John of the Cross, *Dark Night of the Soul* (New York City: Doubleday, 1959).

of faith revealed that less than 1% believed that the Church provided leaders with adequate training to respond to a member's crisis of faith, and only about 4% believed their ward leaders knew how to effectively minister to them in their crises.[4]

In a 2011 interview, Elder Marlin K. Jensen was asked about members of the Church "leaving in droves." He responded, "The fifteen men [of the First Presidency and Quorum of Twelve] really do know, and they really care. And they realize that maybe since Kirtland, we never have had a period of, I'll call it apostasy, like we're having right now."[5] Clearly, crisis of faith in the Church is an important topic that warrants urgent attention.

During a crisis of faith, we may doubt what we once believed was true. We may feel God has abandoned us. Perhaps the solutions we learned in Primary that once renewed our spirit (read your scriptures, say your prayers, attend your church meetings) no longer have an effect. Perhaps we sought counsel from friends, relatives, or Church leaders, but their counsel was inadequate. They may have implied we are to blame for our doubts, which may have caused us to feel guilt and shame.

Perhaps we have considered leaving the Church and abandoning our sacredly held beliefs altogether. To continue in the faith would feel deceitful, even hypocritical. We find ourselves at a crossroads. One path is to abandon all we have held dear: our heritage, traditions, identity, doctrine, hopes, friendships, and even family to foray into a foreign and frightful future. Or we can take the other path and "fake

---

4. David B. Ostler, *Bridges: Ministering to Those Who Question* (Salt Lake City: Greg Kofford Books, 2019), 14.

5. Peter Henderson, "Special report - Mormonism besieged by the modern age," Reuters, Jan. 31, 2012, https://www.reuters.com/article/uk-mormon-church/special-report-mormonism-besieged-by-the-modern-age-idUK-TRE80T1CP20120131.

it till we make it." We can go through the motions hoping our faith will be renewed before we break.

There is, however, another path that lies before us, but it is obscured by our doubt and uncertainty. This path is the best path, the path the Lord intends for us. But it is also the most difficult to follow. This path is the focus of this book, and we will discuss it at length.

A crisis of faith may feel like the death of our testimony. But what if it is *not* the death of our testimony but a rebirth of it?

> *The dark night of the soul is a divinely designed spiritual chrysalis intended to transform us into all the Lord needs us to become and all that we want to become—the best version of us.*

What if a faith crisis is a divinely designed spiritual chrysalis intended to transform us into all the Lord needs us to become and all that we want to become—the best version of us?

Biography

You may be wondering what qualifies me to write about this topic. I am a lifelong member of The Church of Jesus Christ of Latter-day Saints. I served as a missionary in the Kentucky Louisville Mission; was sealed to my wife, Elizabeth, in the Dallas Texas Temple; and have served in many leadership positions in the Church. Though that may be helpful background, it is not what qualifies me to write about crises of faith. What qualifies me is that, after serving a second time as a bishop, I experienced a most severe and devastating crisis of faith, my own dark night of the soul. My experience was painful, frightening, discouraging, and enlightening. What I went through transformed me and filled me with a desire to share what I learned with others in similar crises.

As I emerged from the dark night, I began to study it in depth. I read *The Critical Journey: Stages in the Life of Faith* by Janet O. Hagberg and Robert A. Guelich;[6] *Stages of Faith: The Psychology of Human Development and the Quest for Meaning* by James W. Fowler;[7] *Stages of Faith* by Jon Paulien;[8] *Navigating Mormon Faith Crises: A Simple Developmental Map* by Thomas Wirthlin McConkie;[9] and *Bridges: Ministering to Those Who Question* by David Ostler.[10] Each has shaped my understanding of the stages of faith and faith crises. Many of their ideas influenced this work, though what I present is based on my personal experience and is distinct from their models.

Looking back, I wish I knew then what I know now. I would have been more compassionate, loved more deeply, meted out more mercy, and counseled those in crisis more wisely. Now I share what I learned to help those who are in the depths of the dark night and those who support them.

This work is tailored for members of The Church of Jesus Christ of Latter-day Saints, but it will benefit people of all faiths and religious denominations. The stages of faith apply to all, and crises of faith are common among all who believe in things which are hoped for but not seen (see Hebrews 11:1).

---

6. Janet O. Hagberg and Robert A. Guelich, *The Critical Journey: Stages in the Life of Faith* (Salem, WI: Sheffield Publishing Company, 2005).

7. James Fowler, *Stages of Faith: The Psychology of Human Development and the Quest for Meaning* (New York: HarperCollins Publishers, 1981).

8. Jon Paulien, "The Stages of Faith," The Battle of Armageddon, accessed Nov. 10, 2022, http://thebattleofarmageddon.com/stages_of_faith.html.

9. Thomas Wirthlin McConkie, *Navigating the Mormon Faith Crisis: A Simple Development Map* (Salt Lake City: Mormon Stages, 2015).

10. Ostler, *Bridges.*

Key Points

In this book, we will explore these key points:

- Doubt is not the absence of faith; it is evidence of it.
- There are five stages of faith, and a crisis of faith is associated with each of the first four stages.
- A crisis of faith normally occurs to help us transition to a new stage of spiritual development.
- The dark night of the soul—the crisis of faith at stage three—is the most severe crisis of faith.
- A crisis of faith is divinely designed to transform and refine us.

1

OVERVIEW OF THE STAGES OF FAITH

"The only way to learn strong faith is to endure great trials."

—George Muller[1]

The stages of faith are similar to the stages of human development. Just as we progress physically, emotionally, and mentally from child to adolescent to adult, we similarly progress spiritually through stages as we develop faith. Because the stages of human development are universally familiar, I applied the terms Child, Adolescent, Young Adult, Adult, and Senior to represent the stages of faith.

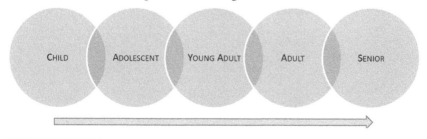

1. George Muller, "The only way," AZ Quotes, accessed Nov. 9, 2022, https://www.azquotes.com/quote/522743.

These terms are universally recognizable, and the stages of faith can parallel the stages of human development. The table on the next page compares these stages with the stages of faith defined by the other authors referenced in this book.

Some people progress spiritually in about the same way they progress physically, emotionally, and mentally, and the stages of faith can be loosely mapped to their age.

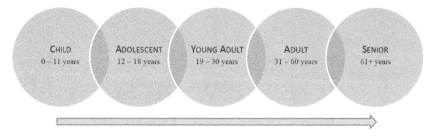

Though many progress though the stages of faith as they age, some who develop faith in childhood may spend much of their lives at a single stage and not progress to the next stage until later in life, if at all. Others find faith later in life and enter the Child stage of faith as adults.

There are a few key points to understand about these stages. First, we progress through each stage in order but can regress in any order. Second, we have a home stage, a stage at which we are most comfortable and may spend much of our life. Third, a crisis of faith most often occurs at the transition point from one stage to the next. The dark night of the soul is one of the transitions.

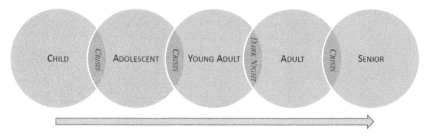

The Dark Night of the Soul Rico Maranto	Stages of Faith James W. Fowler	Navigating Mormon Faith Crisis Thomas Wirthlin McConkie	The Critical Journey Janet Hagberg and Robert Guelich	Stages of Faith Jon Paulien
Child	Intuitive-Projective Faith	Diplomat	The Recognition of God	Initial Acquaintance (Romance)
Adolescent	Mythic-Literal Faith	Expert	The Life of Discipleship	Learning/Discipleship
Young Adult	Synthetic-Conventional Faith	Achiever	The Productive Life	Success
Adult	Individual-Reflective Faith	Individualist	The Journey Inward	Journey Inward
Adult	Conjunctive Faith	Strategist	The Journey Outward	Journey Outward
Senior	Universalizing Faith	Intelligence and the Light of Truth	The Life of Love	Unconditional Love

Fourth, it is not necessary for everyone to progress through the stages. Some may live out their lives at the Child stage; have deep, meaningful relationships with their Father in Heaven and Savior; and receive all the eternal rewards promised to the faithful. Therefore, we need not strive to enter the next stage any more than adolescents should strive to become elderly. We naturally transition when we should and as the Lord wills it; but when He wills it, we must be willing to transition, or we may lose our faith in crisis.

Additionally, one stage is not better or higher than another. For this reason, I hesitate to call them stages for fear the word may imply a hierarchy. Each of us requires different experiences for our spiritual development. Therefore, one may flourish spiritually at the Child stage while another must progress through all the stages of faith to fully develop.

> *We naturally transition when we should and as the Lord wills it; but when He wills it, we must be willing to transition.*

The stages of faith are comparable to medical treatment. In a hospital waiting room, there may be many people with different injuries and ailments. One person may only require an antibiotic, another might need stitches, another requires a cast, and another may need extensive surgery. The one who needs an antibiotic would probably not wish they required surgery. Similarly, the Great Physician diagnoses our spiritual injuries and ailments and prescribes for us a treatment unique to our needs. Some only need to experience the Child stage to fully develop spiritually, while others may need to experience other stages and their associated crises to fully develop.

In later chapters, we will explore each stage of faith in detail. We will consider the characteristics of each stage, what happens as we stagnate at each stage, and the crises of faith we can experience at the transition from one stage to the next. Before we consider the stages in depth, let us consider how each stage satisfies certain needs.

CRISES OF FAITH AND OUR NEEDS

Each stage of faith is associated with a need. A desire to fulfill our needs can spur us to transition to the next stage. At times, our circumstances—or the Lord in His wisdom—deprive us of certain needs. Both desire for and deprivation of our needs can cause a crisis of faith.

The stages of faith parallel Abraham Maslow's hierarchy of needs.[2] Maslow, a psychologist, wrote a paper in 1943 titled "Theory of Human Motivation." In that paper, he proposed that we have certain needs that can be arranged in a hierarchy, with basic needs at the bottom and higher needs at the top. He asserted that we become concerned with higher needs after the lower needs are met. His hierarchy of needs are as follows.

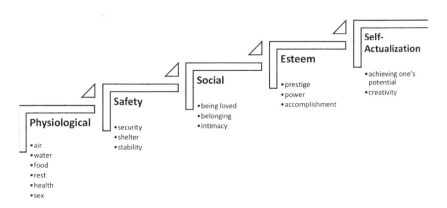

As illustrated, the basic needs are life-sustaining: air, water, food, and rest (Physiological), as well as security, shelter, and stability (Safety). Once those needs are satisfied, we yearn to be loved and

2. See Neel Burton, "Our Hierarchy of Needs," Psychology Today, May 23, 2012, https://www.psychologytoday.com/us/blog/hide-and-seek/201205/our-hierarchy-needs.

belong (Social). Next, we seek accomplishment and desire power, prestige, and recognition (Esteem). Finally, we seek to become the person we have always wanted to be (Self-Actualization).[3]

Each stage of faith is associated with a need in Maslow's hierarchy. Some enter the Child stage of faith when deprived of life-sustaining needs (Physiological) and find in the Church security, shelter, and stability (Safety). We then want to belong, to be included in the church community (Social), which causes us to transition to the Adolescent stage of faith. Next, we want more than to just belong—we want to contribute and to be needed in the community. This need spurs us into the Young Adult stage of faith. Finally, we transition through the Adult and Senior stages of faith and "go beyond our individual, limited selves" to "fulfil our true potential"[4] (Self-Actualization). In this way, we transcend beyond our selfish needs and desires and "embark in the service of God . . . with an eye single to [His] glory" (Doctrine and Covenants 4:2, 5). Our desires align with the Lord's desires. We no longer care to become what we want to become; we now want to become who *He* wants to us to become.

Sometimes, in the Lord's wisdom, He deprives us of our needs in order to spur us to the next stage of faith. For example, he said, "How oft have I called upon you by the mouth of my servants, and by the ministering of angels, and by mine own voice, and by the voice of thunderings, and by the voice of lightnings, and by the voice of tempests, and by the voice of earthquakes, and great hailstorms, and by the voice of famines and pestilences of every kind" (Doctrine and Covenants 43:25).

---

3. See Kendra Cherry, "Maslow's Hierarchy of Needs," Very Well Mind, last modified Aug. 14, 2022, https://www.verywellmind.com/what-is-maslows-hierarchy-of-needs-4136760.

4. Burton, "Our Hierarchy of Needs."

Sometimes he calls to us with thunderings, lightnings, tempests, earthquakes, hailstorms, famines, and pestilences. He deprives us of life-sustaining needs and strips us of safety, shelter, and stability to spur us to the next stage of faith.

A good example of this is in the book of Helaman. The Nephites had rejected the words of the prophets and had fallen into a state of "awful wickedness" (Helaman 7:4). In Helaman 11, we read that they were at war with the Gadianton robbers who were on the verge of defeating them. Nephi begged the Lord not to allow the Gadianton robbers to destroy the people but asked that they suffer famine instead, hoping they would remember the Lord, repent, and return to Him. So the Lord caused a famine, and when the people were about to perish, they remembered the Lord and repented. He then sent the rains, and the earth again "did bring forth her fruit" (verse 17) and "the people did rejoice and glorify God" (verse 18).

Like the Nephites, when we are deprived of a need, our circumstances can spur us to transition to the next stage of faith. Perhaps we are unemployed, suffering illness, or otherwise unable to secure the necessities of life (Physiological). Perhaps we are going through a divorce or have been betrayed by a friend and feel vulnerable and unstable (Safety). Perhaps we are passed over for a promotion or a business venture fails (Esteem). We are "brought low through oppression, affliction, and sorrow" (Psalm 107:30). The circumstances humble us and, in our anxious search for solutions, we may cry unto the Lord in our trouble (see Psalm 107:6) and turn to Him "who redeemeth [our lives] from destruction; who crowneth [us] with lovingkindness and tender mercies" (Psalm 103:4).

Just as He, at times, deprives us of some needs, He likewise promises to fulfill our needs. He appeals to our Esteem needs with promises of "glory and honor and the riches of eternal life" (Doctrine and Covenants 43:25), and He promises Self-Actualization through exaltation.

A crisis of faith most often occurs when we perceive that our faith or the Church is depriving us of a need. When we are deprived of a need, we may conclude that our faith is flawed or the Church is a fraud and then plunge into the dark night of the soul. Perhaps we are struggling to feed our family (Physiological) and tithing is an unfair burden. Perhaps a change in Church policy shakes our stability (Safety). Perhaps we feel we do not fit in or that the Church's position on a social issue excludes someone we love, dividing our church community from our family/friend community (Social). Perhaps we discover a doctrine that does not resonate with us, or an event in Church history that offends our values, and this causes us to question whether we still belong in the Church (Social). Perhaps we are passed over for a leadership calling or not considered for what we perceive to be weightier responsibilities, which can wear down our self-esteem (Esteem). Perhaps we doubt we can be "perfect in Christ" (Moroni 10:32) or give all that is expected because the sacrifice is too great and may prevent us from pursuing our personal ambitions (Self-Actualization). After all, Joseph Smith said:

A crisis of faith most often occurs when we perceive that our faith or the Church is depriving us of a need.

> Let us here observe that a religion that does not require the sacrifice of all things never has power sufficient to produce the faith necessary unto life and salvation. For from the first existence of man, the faith necessary unto the enjoyment of life and salvation never could be obtained without the sacrifice of all earthly things. It is through this sacrifice, and this only, that God has ordained that men should enjoy eternal life. And it is through the medium of the sacrifice of

all earthly things that men do actually know that they are doing the things that are well pleasing in the sight of God.[5]

Christ perfects us through His atonement as we sacrifice our needs and desires. In fact, the term sacrifice derives from the Latin word *sacer*, meaning sacred or holy, and *facere*, meaning to make. Therefore, sacrifice means *to make holy*.[6] We become holy as we learn to lay our needs and desires on the sacrificial altar. Elder Neal A. Maxwell once taught:

> The submission of one's will is really the only uniquely personal thing we have to place on God's altar. The many other things we "give," brothers and sisters, are actually the things He has already given or loaned to us. However, when you and I finally submit ourselves, by letting our individual wills be swallowed up in God's will, then we are really giving something to Him! It is the only possession which is truly ours to give!
>
> Consecration thus constitutes the only unconditional surrender which is also a total victory![7]

Striving to abstain from sin is sacrificing our needs, for all sins are rooted in our desire to satisfy one or more needs in Maslow's hierarchy. Consider Jesus's experience when Satan tempted Him in the wilderness. He had been fasting "forty days and forty nights, [and] he was afterward an hungered" (Matthew 4:2). Satan tempted Him to turn stones into bread and eat (Physiological). Then Satan tempted Him to throw Himself off the pinnacle of the temple to see if angels would save Him (Safety). After that, Satan took Him up "into an exceeding high mountain, and sheweth him all the kingdoms of the

---

5. *Lectures on Faith* [1985], 59–60.

6. See "Sacrifice: Making Yourself Sacred," J. Marshall Jenkins, Feb. 15, 2017, https://www.jmarshalljenkins.com/2017/02/15/sacrifice-making-sacred-lent-life/.

7. Neal A. Maxwell, "'Swallowed Up in the Will of the Father,'" *Ensign*, Nov. 1995, 24.

world, and the glory of them; And saith unto him, All these things will I give thee, if thou wilt fall down and worship me" (Matthew 4:8–9) (Esteem, Self-Actualization). Satan progressively tempted Jesus at each level in Maslow's hierarchy. He knows human nature and leverages our needs to distill within us the desire for sin.

Conversely, consider the covenants we make in the temple. Each covenant, made at an altar, is a call to sacrifice something of our needs, wants, and desires. We covenant to be chaste and keep any sexual relations within the bounds of marriage (Physiological). We covenant to avoid light-mindedness, frivolity, and gossip (Social). We covenant to consecrate all that we possess for the building up of the kingdom of God (Physiological, Safety, Social, Esteem, Self-Actualization).

As we sacrifice, we are endowed—gifted—from on high. As we give, the Lord gives. And if we sacrifice all we have, that minuscule amount might do little for the Lord and the Church, but it will do everything for us because sacrifice makes us holy. We can become "heirs of God, and joint-heirs with Christ" (Romans 8:17); "inherit thrones, kingdoms, principalities, and powers, dominions, all heights and depths" (Doctrine and Covenants 132:19); and receive all that the Father has (see Doctrine and Covenants 84:38).

Ironically, it is the sacrifice of all things that gives us all things. Consider the Savior's counsel and promise in Matthew 6:

> And your heavenly Father will provide for you, whatsoever things ye need for food, what ye shall eat; and for raiment, what ye shall wear or put on. (Joseph Smith Translation, Matthew 6:27 [in Matthew 6:25, footnote a])
>
> Therefore take no thought, saying, What shall we eat? or, What shall we drink? or, Wherewithal shall we be clothed? . . . For your heavenly Father knoweth that ye have need of all these things. (Matthew 26:31–32)
>
> Wherefore, seek not the things of this world but seek ye first to build up the kingdom of God, and to establish his righteousness,

and all these things shall be added unto you. (Joseph Smith Translation, Matthew 6:38 [in Matthew 6:33, footnote *a*])

As we sacrifice to build His kingdom, God builds *our* kingdom. He provides for our needs when we sacrifice to provide for His needs. He requires our time, talents, energy, and possessions to build His kingdom and bless those we serve. Such sacrifice requires faith—something that is in short supply when we are experiencing a crisis of faith.

As an example of such faith, allow me to share a personal story. A long time ago, I befriended a squirrel. He would sit on my lap and eat nuts from my hand. Years later, I was sitting on my front stoop and decided to befriend another squirrel. As he scurried about looking for a nut, I tossed a peanut in his vicinity. He cautiously sniffed it out, took it into his little paws, and nibbled eagerly until he devoured it. As he ate, he eyed me warily, unsure whether I was a provider or a predator. I continued to toss out peanuts, bringing him closer and closer to me until his fear of me superceded his hunger. On that first day, he kept a distance of about ten feet.

At that time, I was emerging from the dark night of the soul. One of the contributing factors that darkened my dark night was the loss of my job. I had been unemployed for nearly a year. Our savings were nearly depleted, and my employment prospects looked grim. I was applying for every relevant position, interviewing regularly, and networking, and I even started a business in an effort to provide for my family. All to no avail. As I sat on the front stoop befriending that squirrel, I pondered how I would provide for my family when our savings ran out, fearing I would have to withdraw from my 401K, incurring onerous taxes and penalties and depleting my retirement savings.

I tossed the squirrel peanuts each day for the next two weeks. Before I tossed a peanut, I would shake the can a little so he would learn that the sound indicated he was about to be fed. Each day he would come closer and closer to me. At the end of two weeks, he sat almost within arm's reach. I was certain that on the next day he would eat from my hand.

The next day I found him scurrying about, so I shook the peanut can. I then tossed a peanut about five feet from me. He continued to scurry about. I shook the can again. And again. The squirrel ignored me and continued scurrying about. I sat there bewildered. I thought to myself, *Why is this silly squirrel scurrying about trying to eke out a nut when I am here to give him more nuts than he can ever eat? All he needs to do is come to me.*

Then the Spirit spoke to me in a still, small voice: "You are a lot like that squirrel. You scurry about trying to eke out a living when 'your heavenly Father knoweth that ye have need of all these things. Wherefore, seek not the things of this world but seek ye first to build up the kingdom of God, and to establish his righteousness, and all these things shall be added unto you.' All you need to do is come unto me."

Convicted, I knew that if I were to build the kingdom of God, I needed to start with myself. I gradually turned to the Lord. I prayed a little. I pondered a little. I listened to the scriptures on audio every now and then. Those things did not bring me out of the dark night as some might suppose. Instead, I felt some desire for those things as I emerged from the dark night. I could feel my heart softening and a subtle yearning to reconnect with my Father in Heaven. It was like eating during an illness, where the illness causes a loss of appetite. We may not want to eat while we are sick, but our appetite gradually returns as we get better. Then, as we eat, we become stronger and recover.

At one point, I shared my testimony in fast and testimony meeting, something I rarely did during my long dark night. After the meeting, as we exited the chapel, someone called to me in the hall. I looked in the direction of the voice and discovered it was Debbie, a friend I had not seen in over fifteen years. We were in the same ward in Colorado, and for about a year, I had worked for her husband, Steve, at his company. (Coincidentally, it was during that year that I had befriended the first squirrel.)

She explained that they had just moved to Houston and were not sure what ward they were in, so they just picked one to attend for the day. We later learned that their ward was in a different building. We talked briefly and promised to get together once they settled in.

A few weeks later, Steve called me and explained that his company had merged with another company. He said they were growing and asked if I would be interested in a job opportunity. I explained I had been unemployed for some time and was very interested. A week later, I had a job.

The Lord provided what I needed when I sought first to build the kingdom of God. Bearing my fragile testimony was a simple act of faith that signaled my intent to build His kingdom. For that, He did "immediately bless [me]" (Mosiah 2:24).

A crisis of faith often derives from a desire for or deprivation of a need.

In summary, the stages of faith are closely related to Maslow's hierarchy of needs. Our evolving desire for higher-level needs can cause us to transition to the next stage of faith. Sometimes, our circumstances, or the Lord in His wisdom, deprive us of a need, spurring us to transition to another stage of faith. Therefore, a crisis of faith often derives from a desire for or deprivation of a need. This is often the catalyst that causes the transition and resulting spiritual growth. Throughout this book, we will discuss the various needs at each stage of faith and how they can cause crises of faith.

Key Point Summary

- There are five stages of faith.
- Crises of faith often occur at the transition point between stages.
- Crises are typically rooted in an unfulfilled need.

2

Faith and Doubt

"Doubt is not the opposite of faith; it is an element of faith. . . . Sometimes I think it is my mission to bring faith to the faithless, and doubt to the faithful."

—Paul Tillich[1]

In order to understand a crisis of faith, we must first understand that doubt is an essential characteristic of faith. We have been taught that faith is to believe and not doubt. For example, the Savior said to his disciples, "If ye have faith, and doubt not . . . whatsoever ye shall ask in prayer, believing, ye shall receive" (Matthew 21:21–22). When Peter tried to walk on water and began to sink, Jesus compassionately rescued him and asked, "O thou of little faith, wherefore didst thou doubt?" (Matthew 14:31). In the Book of Mormon, we learn of the two thousand stripling warriors who were miraculously preserved because of "their exceeding faith" and because they "did not doubt" (Alma 57:26). *Lectures on Faith* states, "Where doubt and uncertainty

---

1. Paul Tillich, "Sometimes I think," AZ Quotes, accessed Nov. 12, 2022, https://www.azquotes.com/quote/415289.

are, there faith is not, nor can it be. For doubt and faith do not exist in the same person at the same time."[2]

Because of examples and teachings like these, some believe that doubt is the absence of faith. Then, when we feel doubts—as we do in a crisis of faith—we may think we doubt because our faith is insufficient. We may tell ourselves, or perhaps others tell us, that we doubt because we lack faith or are choosing to not believe. We then feel guilt and shame.

But doubt is not the absence of faith; it is evidence of it. Faith and doubt are two sides of the same coin. Thomas McConkie explained, "It is not by banishing doubt that we ultimately resolve the tension with faith, but by bringing the two into a deeper synthesis. In this joining of opposites, we lay the foundation for yet higher stages of development."[3] Since faith and doubt are inseparably connected, we should not feel guilt and shame when we doubt. Therefore, doubt and shame should not be companion emotions.

Doubt is not the absence of faith; it is evidence of it.

In Alma 32:21, we read that "faith is not to have a perfect knowledge"; it is to "hope for things which are not seen." In other words, *to have faith is to doubt*—to not know—but to *hope* for those things we cannot prove. Moroni explained that after the brother of Jared saw the Lord, "he had faith no longer, for he knew, nothing doubting" (Ether 3:19), implying that before that vision, he had faith *and* doubts.

So, does faith include doubt, or does it mean to doubt not? How do we reconcile these seemingly conflicting ideas about faith? Joseph Smith described faith as "hope [you have], in consequence of your

2. *Lectures on Faith* (1985), 62.

3. Thomas Wirthlin McConkie, *Navigating the Mormon Faith Crisis: A Simple Development Map* (Salt Lake City: Mormon Stages, 2015), 101.

belief in the existence of unseen things, which [stimulate] you to action and exertion in order to obtain them. . . . Faith is . . . the moving cause of all action in yourselves."[4]

Therefore, faith is acting on hope and belief. Thus, one definition of faith is *hope and belief in action*. Faith is acting as if we are certain what we want to believe is true, even if we have some doubts.

> *Doubt and shame should not be companion emotions.*

When we define faith as hope and belief in action, we can reconcile the conflicting ideas that (1) faith is to not doubt and (2) doubt is the evidence of faith. They are reconciled when we interpret the counsel to "doubt not" to mean that we should act in faith despite our doubts—to act as if we have no doubts.

We exercise faith and "doubt not" every day in everything we do. We exercise faith when we walk into a dark room and flip the light switch. We don't know if the light will turn on, but we believe it will, so we flip the switch. Each time we sit in a chair, we don't know if the chair will support us, but we believe it will, so we sit down.

My family has three cars. My wife and I each have a car, and we also have a Jeep that our sons share. During the COVID-19 lockdown in 2020, that Jeep sat idle for months. One day we needed to move the Jeep. I knew the battery was probably dead, but I didn't want to drive my truck over to it, open the hoods, and hook up the jumper cables if I didn't have to. So, I hoped the Jeep would start. I put the key in the ignition and turned it. The car was a bit sluggish, but it started.

That was faith! Faith began by hoping the Jeep would start so I wouldn't have to jump it. That hope led to the belief that it was worthwhile to try starting it, even though I doubted it would start. That belief became faith when I turned the key. And when the car started, I no longer had faith because I had a perfect knowledge.

---

4. *Lectures on Faith* (1985), 2.

Hope leads to belief. Belief leads to action. Faith is belief in action. To "doubt not" is to act in faith despite our doubts—to act as if we have no doubts. And when we do, that faith eventually becomes a perfect knowledge (see Alma 32:34).

Flipping a light switch, sitting in a chair, and starting a car are simple acts of faith bolstered by the fact we have previously done each with successful results. Faith in Christ and His gospel is not quite so simple. At times, we must believe and act without results. We flip the switch through prayer and see no light, we move to the chair where we think the Lord wants us to sit and it collapses under us, we start the car and continue down the road we feel the Lord wants us to take and then find ourselves lost. Such is the journey of faith. Each step forward can be a step into the darkness, for we receive no witness until after the trial of our faith (see Ether 12:6). Eventually, in the Lord's time, the light breaks through the darkness; He lifts us by the hand and shows us the way.

Now that we have discussed faith and doubt, let us consider the seasons of faith.

Seasons of Faith

Alma, during his mission to the Zoramites, gave a preeminent lecture on faith recorded in Alma 32. In that lecture, he compared faith to a seed.

> Now, we will compare the word unto a seed. Now, if ye give place, that a seed may be planted in your heart, behold, if it be a true seed, or a good seed, if ye do not cast it out by your unbelief, that ye will resist the Spirit of the Lord, behold, it will begin to swell within your breasts; and when you feel these swelling motions, ye will begin to say within yourselves—It must needs be that this is a good seed, or that the word is good, for it beginneth to enlarge

my soul; yea, it beginneth to enlighten my understanding, yea, it beginneth to be delicious to me.

But behold, as the seed swelleth, and sprouteth, and beginneth to grow, then you must needs say that the seed is good; for behold it swelleth, and sprouteth, and beginneth to grow. And now, behold, will not this strengthen your faith? Yea, it will strengthen your faith: for ye will say I know that this is a good seed; for behold it sprouteth and beginneth to grow.

And behold, as the tree beginneth to grow, ye will say: Let us nourish it with great care, that it may get root, that it may grow up, and bring forth fruit unto us. And now behold, if ye nourish it with much care it will get root, and grow up, and bring forth fruit.

But if ye will nourish the word, yea, nourish the tree as it beginneth to grow, by your faith with great diligence, and with patience, looking forward to the fruit thereof, it shall take root; and behold it shall be a tree springing up unto everlasting life.

And because of your diligence and your faith and your patience with the word in nourishing it, that it may take root in you, behold, by and by ye shall pluck the fruit thereof, which is most precious, which is sweet above all that is sweet, and which is white above all that is white, yea, and pure above all that is pure; and ye shall feast upon this fruit even until ye are filled, that ye hunger not, neither shall ye thirst. (Alma 32:28, 30, 37–42)

In these verses, Alma describes one's faith as a tiny seed that grows into a fruitful tree. His instruction to nourish it with great care, diligence, and patience reminds us that faith does not grow spontaneously but by the sweat of our brow amidst thorns and thistles.

Though not mentioned, we understand that the tender plant passes through different seasons. The growth Alma describes occurs in the spring, when conditions are

> *Faith does not grow spontaneously but by the sweat of our brow amidst thorns and thistles.*

ideal. In the springs of life, our testimony blossoms and our faith is certain—almost a sure knowledge.

Alma explains how our faith transitions from belief to a sure knowledge:

> If it be a true seed, or a good seed, if ye do not cast it out by your unbelief, that ye will resist the Spirit of the Lord, behold, it will begin to swell within your breasts; and when you feel these swelling motions, ye will begin to say within yourselves—It must needs be that this is a good seed, or that the word is good, for it beginneth to enlarge my soul; yea, it beginneth to enlighten my understanding, yea, it beginneth to be delicious to me. (Alma 32:28)

Our faith increases when we "feel these swelling motions," as if our soul is enlarged. Our understanding is enlightened and we crave the word of God. In Doctrine and Covenants 121:42, we learn that pure knowledge greatly enlarges the soul. Some associate the warm feeling that accompanies the swelling in the breast with the burning of the bosom the Savior described to Oliver Cowdery. He said, "You must study it out in your mind; then you must ask me if it be right, and if it is right I will cause that your bosom shall burn within you; therefore, you shall feel that it is right" (Doctrine and Covenants 9:8). The two men who walked with the resurrected Lord on the road to Emmaus experienced this burning in the bosom. They recalled, "Did not our heart burn within us, while he talked with us by the way, and while he opened to us the scriptures?" (Luke 24:32).

This enlargement of the soul feels like our spirit is swelling within us. Our spirit is invigorated by the nourishing fruit of the Spirit—love and its companion emotions joy and peace (see Galatians 5:22)—"proving what is acceptable unto the Lord" (Ephesians 5:10). We feel a warmth grow within us as we are encircled by His love and are enlightened by the pure knowledge imparted when Spirit speaks to spirit, the purest form of communication—communication unencumbered by weak words.

Alma continues, "Now behold, would not this increase your faith? I say unto you, Yea; nevertheless it hath not grown up to a perfect knowledge" (Alma 32:29).

The powerful witness Alma describes in verse 28 increases our faith, but it is not a perfect knowledge and does not dispel all doubts. He continues:

> But behold, as the seed swelleth, and sprouteth, and beginneth to grow, then you must needs say that the seed is good; for behold it swelleth, and sprouteth, and beginneth to grow. And now, behold, will not this strengthen your faith? Yea, it will strengthen your faith: for ye will say I know that this is a good seed; for behold it sprouteth and beginneth to grow.
>
> And now, behold, because ye have tried the experiment, and planted the seed, and it swelleth and sprouteth, and beginneth to grow, ye must needs know that the seed is good.
>
> And now, behold, is your knowledge perfect? Yea, your knowledge is perfect in that thing, and your faith is dormant; and this because you know, for ye know that the word hath swelled your souls, and ye also know that it hath sprouted up, that your understanding doth begin to be enlightened, and your mind doth begin to expand. (Alma 32:30, 33–34)

Here, Alma explains that the witness we have received makes our knowledge "perfect in that thing." He is teaching us that we can have a sure testimony of a single truth of the gospel while remaining uncertain about everything else. We can *know* one thing is true while doubting all else.

When I was a new full-time missionary serving in my first area—Prestonsburg, Kentucky—my companion and I were invited to a member's home to watch a broadcast from Salt Lake commemorating

President Ezra Taft Benson's ninetieth birthday.[5] Satellite television was a new technology, and this member was one of the few people in the small town who had a satellite dish at his home.

I watched the event with interest. Gordon B. Hinckley, who was serving as President Benson's first counselor, was the concluding speaker. At the end of his remarks, he asked Thomas S. Monson, second counselor, to help President Benson to the pulpit. The aged President Benson was stooped and unsteady as he shuffled to the pulpit. His frame was frail, and he leaned heavily on President Monson's arm.

Presidents Hinckley and Monson presented him a gift—a leather-bound book that contained sentiments from each of them and the members of the Quorum of the Twelve.

They then asked President Benson if he would like to say something. I leaned forward, excited to hear the prophet's counsel. He haltingly began to speak; his age had clearly taken a toll on his mind. There were long, awkward, mid-sentence pauses. At one point he started a sentence, and then, as if he forgot what he was saying, he stopped talking and began thumbing clumsily through the book. President Monson had to help him turn the pages.

I thought to myself, *I'm supposed to spend two years of my life testifying that this old man is a prophet and the mouthpiece of God? He can hardly form a complete sentence!* I then said a silent prayer that was more the demand of an obstinate adolescent than supplication of a submissive child. *Father, I need to know right now if this man is a prophet!*

Instantly, I was reminded of the story of Balaam in the Old Testament. The fact that I remembered this obscure story was in itself

---

5. See Hard-to-Find Mormon Videos, "President Benson's 90th Birthday Celebration (1989)," Oct. 17, 2016, https://www.youtube.com/watch?v=_n4MagZ9erU.

a miracle. It was inspiration from the Holy Ghost, "who brings all things to [our] remembrance" (John 14:26). Balaam, who had disobeyed the Lord, was riding his donkey on a narrow path between two walls. An angel stood in the way with his sword drawn. The donkey could see the angel, but Balaam could not. To avoid the angel, the donkey pressed into one of the walls, crushing Balaam's foot. Angered, Balaam hit her with his staff. The donkey, unable to move forward because of the angel but not wanting Balaam to strike her again, sunk down to the ground, whereupon Balaam struck her again.

Then the Lord opened the donkey's mouth and the donkey said to Balaam, "What have I done unto thee, that thou hast smitten me?" (Numbers 22:28).

Balaam replied, "Because thou hast mocked me: I would there were a sword in mine hand, for now would I kill thee" (verse 29).

The donkey countered, "Am not I thine . . . upon which thou hast ridden ever since I was thine unto this day? Was I ever wont to do so unto thee?" (verse 30).

Balaam admitted she had never done that before. Then the Lord opened Balaam's eyes, and he saw the angel standing in their way with his sword drawn. Balaam then bowed himself to the ground and humbly received the angel's chastisement.

After recalling Balaam's story, the Lord—in that still, small voice that pierces the soul—firmly but gently rebuked me: "If I can give utterance to a donkey, I can give utterance to an old man. Right now, I don't need him to speak as a prophet. But if I did, he would speak with great power and authority."

In that moment, my mind was enlightened, my spirit swelled in my chest, and tears streamed down my cheeks as I basked in the warmth of the Father's infinite love and the kindness of His gentle rebuke.

From that moment, I *knew* Ezra Taft Benson was a prophet of God. "I knew it, and I knew that God knew it, and I could not deny it, neither dared I do it; at least I knew that by so doing I would offend God, and come under condemnation" (Joseph Smith—History 1:25). I had a perfect knowledge "in that thing" (Alma 32:34) and my faith was dormant.

Since that time, other great men have served as presidents of The Church of Jesus Christ of Latter-day Saints: Howard W. Hunter, Gordon B. Hinckley, Thomas S. Monson, and, at present, Russell M. Nelson. I *believe* all these men are prophets, seers, and revelators, but I don't *know* it. I have not received a similarly powerful witness that would make my "knowledge perfect" (Alma 32:34) regarding these men. But I *believe* they are prophets and demonstrate my faith by acting on that belief. Therefore, we can have a sure testimony of one thing and remain uncertain about other things.

Unanswered Prayers

One whose prayers seem to go unanswered in the midst of a crisis of faith may wonder why the answer to my question came so swiftly. Comparably, one might consider why it was that Joseph Smith barely uttered a few words in prayer and triggered supernatural events, while Enos prayed all day and all night before hearing the voice of the Lord.

Consider Lorenzo Snow's experience. President Wilford Woodruff's health was failing, and he was not expected to live much longer. Lorenzo Snow, who was then the President of the Council of Twelve, was worried about succeeding President Woodruff, in part because of the Church's dire financial circumstances.

In his room in the Salt Lake Temple, he dressed in the robes of the priesthood and then went to the Holy of Holies. He knelt at the altar and prayed fervently:

He [pled] with the Lord to spare President Woodruff's life, that President Woodruff might outlive him, and that the great responsibility of Church leadership would never fall upon his shoulders. Yet he promised the Lord that he would devotedly perform any duty required at his hands.[6]

Soon after, President Woodruff died, prompting President Snow to return to the temple.

President Snow put on his holy temple robes, repaired again to the same sacred altar, offered up the signs of the Priesthood, and poured out his heart to the Lord. He reminded the Lord how he had [pled] for President Woodruff's life and that his days might be lengthened beyond his own; that he might never be called upon to bear the heavy burdens and responsibilities of Church leadership. "Nevertheless," he said, "Thy will be done. I have not sought this responsibility but if it be Thy will, I now present myself before Thee for Thy guidance and instruction. I ask that Thou show me what Thou wouldst have me do."

After finishing his prayer he expected a reply, some special manifestation from the Lord. So he waited—and waited—and waited. There was no reply, no voice, no visitation, no manifestation. He left the altar and the room in great disappointment.[7]

Lorenzo Snow was a prophet, seer, and revelator, the President of the Quorum of the Twelve Apostles, and soon to be set apart as the next President of the Church. If anyone was worthy of a swift and direct response from the Lord, he was. Yet there was no answer. The heavens were silent, and he was left alone to ponder why.

Three days passed with no answer.[8] Then the answer came.

---

6. N. B. Lundwall, *Temples of the Most High* (Salt Lake City: Bookcraft, 1941), 140.

7. Lundwall, *Temples of the Most High*, 140–41.

8. See Lawrence R. Flake, *Prophets and Apostles of the Last Dispensation* (Provo, UT: Religious Studies Center, Brigham Young University, 2001), 55.

Some time thereafter, he shared his experience with his grand-daughter, Allie Young Pond. She later recounted:

> One evening when I was visiting Grandpa Snow in his room in the
> Salt Lake Temple, I remained until the doorkeepers had gone and
> the nightwatchman had not yet come in, so Grandpa said he would
> take me to the main front entrance and let me out that way. He got
> his bunch of keys from his dresser.
>
> After we left his room and while we were still in the large
> corridor, leading into the Celestial room, I was walking several steps
> ahead of Grandpa when he stopped me, saying: "Wait a moment,
> Allie. I want to tell you something. It was right here that the Lord
> Jesus Christ appeared to me at the time of the death of President
> Woodruff. He instructed me to go right ahead and reorganize the
> First Presidency of the Church at once and not wait as he had done
> after the death of the previous presidents, and that I was to succeed
> President Woodruff."
>
> Then Grandpa came a step nearer and held out his left hand
> and said: "He stood right here, about three feet above the floor. It
> looked as though He stood on a plate of solid gold."
>
> Grandpa told me what a glorious personage the Savior is and
> described His hands, feet, countenance and beautiful White Robes,
> all of which were of such a glory of whiteness and brightness that he
> could hardly gaze upon Him.
>
> Then Grandpa came another step nearer me and put his right
> hand on my head and said: "Now, granddaughter, I want you to
> remember that this is the testimony of your grandfather, that he
> told you with his own lips that he actually saw the Savior here in
> the Temple and talked with Him face to face."
>
> Then we went on and Grandpa let me out of the main front
> door of the Temple. [9]

Why does the Lord answer some immediately and leave others to
wait days, months, or even years for an answer? We especially need answers when we are experiencing a crisis of faith. Should not our Father

---

9. Lundwall, *Temples of the Most High*, 141.

in Heaven more quickly respond to the pleadings of a lost child? Did not the Lord promise to answer us? "Ask, and it shall be given you; seek, and ye shall find; knock, and it shall be opened unto you. For every one that asketh receiveth; and he that seeketh findeth; and to him that knocketh it shall be opened" (Luke 11:9–10).

It is difficult to comprehend why He might delay an answer to a heartfelt, humble prayer. In the movie *Rudy*, Father Cavanaugh explained to Rudy that "praying is something we do in our time; the answers come in God's time."[10] We must remember that all things are "done in the wisdom of him who knoweth all things" (2 Nephi 2:24) "which are to come" (Words of Mormon 1:7). He reminds us, "For my thoughts are not your thoughts, neither are your ways my ways, saith the Lord. For as the heavens are higher than the earth, so are my ways higher than your ways, and my thoughts than your thoughts" (Isaiah 55:8–9).

There are a number of reasons answers may not come when we would like. Perhaps we are not ready to receive the answer because the Lord requires something difficult of us and wants to give us time to prepare. Perhaps He is pausing to verify we have "real intent" (Moroni 10:4) and that we will do whatever is required when He gives the answer. Perhaps there is sin in our life that distances the Spirit and makes it difficult for us to hear His voice. Nephi explained to Laman and Lemuel that the Lord had "spoken unto [them] in a still small voice, but [they] were past feeling, that [they] could not feel his words" (1 Nephi 17:45). Perhaps the Lord wants us to labor more for the answer. When Oliver Cowdery was frustrated that he was unable to translate the Book of Mormon, the Lord explained to him, as noted earlier, "You must study it out in your mind; then you must ask me if it be right" (Doctrine and Covenants 9:8). The Lord may withhold

---

10. *Rudy*, directed by David Anspaugh (TriStar Pictures, 1993), https://www. netflix.com/title/60002332.

the answer so that it is sweeter when it comes. Perhaps the Lord knows that the circumstances will soon evolve, resolving the issue. Regardless of the reason, we can rest assured that His delay is ultimately for our good and benefit (see Doctrine and Covenants 122:7).

Seasons of Faith

In the spring of our faith, our testimony blossoms. But what about fall, summer, and winter? In summer, we are tried in the heat of adversity. In fall, we sense the coming winter, and like the leaves, our once vivid image of our convictions lose their color. The truths we clung to hang tenuously and one by one begin to drop from certainty to uncertainty. Then the cold winter comes, and the warmth we enjoyed in spring is a distant memory—or was it imagined? Our testimony is dormant, and we question whether there is life still in it.

Some of earth's seasons seem milder or harsher than the same season in prior years. Some seasons seem shorter while others seem longer. Even within a season, some days are warmer than others, rains may or may not fall, and so on. In some climates, summers are unbearable while winters are pleasant and vice versa. Similarly, the seasons of faith can differ from person to person, and the same person can experience the same season differently. For one, a season of faith can last hours, and for another it can last years. Winters are mild for one person and harsh for another. One might dwell in never-ending winter while another glides through life in perpetual spring. One might experience the seasons in order and another in a different order. Each of us experiences our journey of faith differently because our Father in Heaven tailors the events in our lives to work together for our good (see Doctrine and Covenants 90:24; 122:7).

A winter of faith is a crisis of faith; however, it may not be *the* crisis of faith. Winters of faith prepare us for *the* crisis of faith, which is the darkest night of the coldest winter. It is most easily recognized by those who are experiencing it or have experienced it. Others who have not yet experienced the dark night may fear that a winter of their faith is the death of their testimony. But as they nourish the seed with great care, diligence, and patience, they may enjoy a few sunny days in the winter until spring restores them.

> *In the dark night, the disciplines that once nourished and restored our faith may no longer work.*

A primary difference between a winter of faith and the dark night of the soul is that, in the dark night, the disciplines that once nourished and restored our faith may no longer work. The solutions we learned in Primary—read your scriptures, say your prayers, go to church, and so on—may no longer renew us. These solutions we learned as children, as essential as they are, may be insufficient to save us from the dark night we experience as adults.

It should be noted that while seasons are imposed upon us, nourishment depends on us. We cannot prevent adversity in the heat of summer, but we *can* nourish our faith in order to prepare for it. Our faith cannot survive it if we have neglected to nourish the seed. Alma explained:

> But if ye neglect the tree, and take no thought for its nourishment, behold it will not get any root; and when the heat of the sun cometh and scorcheth it, because it hath no root it withers away, and ye pluck it up and cast it out.
>
> Now, this is not because the seed was not good, neither is it because the fruit thereof would not be desirable; but it is because your ground is barren, and ye will not nourish the tree, therefore ye cannot have the fruit thereof.
>
> And thus, if ye will not nourish the word, looking forward with an eye of faith to the fruit thereof, ye can never pluck of the fruit of the tree of life. (Alma 32:38–40)

If we find our testimony weakened, we must critically assess how well we have nourished the seed. We must ask ourselves whether our faith is weak because of a shift in season or whether we may have weakened it through our own negligence. For this reason, when we seek counsel in a crisis of faith, wise bishops and confidants may ask us if we are reading our scriptures, saying our prayers, keeping the commandments, and so forth, because these disciplines nourish our testimony and can restore our faith. On the other hand, neglecting to nourish our faith will kill it regardless of the season. Elder M. Russell Ballard explained:

> *If we find our testimony weakened, we must critically assess how well we have nourished the seed. Neglecting to nourish our faith will kill it regardless of the season.*

> When someone stops doing these simple but essential things, they cut themselves off from the well of living water and allow Satan to muddy their thinking with his deceptively polluted water, which clogs arteries of faithfulness and drains the spirit with counterfeit nutrition. Sin and guilt cloud the mind—leading many to deny past inspiration and revelation and causing a "de-conversion" from the truths of the gospel of Jesus Christ.[11]

Another difference between winters of faith and the dark night of the soul is that the winters of faith come in cycles whereas the dark night is an event. Each of us will experience ebbs and flows of faith in the course of life as events strengthen or weaken our faith, but the dark night is a divinely appointed event that occurs on the Lord's timeline in the Lord's way. Even one who has diligently practiced the nourishing disciplines may be thrust into the dark night. As a result, they may feel God has abandoned them or question whether He was ever there.

---

11. M. Russell Ballard, "An Epistle from an Apostle," *Liahona*, Sept. 2019.

Now that we have discussed faith, the seasons of faith, and how doubt is the evidence of faith, we will explore the stages of faith and the purpose of the dark night of the soul.

KEY POINT SUMMARY

- Feeling doubt is not the absence of faith; it is evidence of faith.
- Faith is acting on hope and belief despite our doubts.
- There are seasons of faith in which faith can flourish or be dormant.

3

THE CHILD STAGE OF FAITH

"I realized that my life was to be one of simple, childlike
faith, and that my part was to trust, not to do. I was to trust
in Him and He would work in me to do His good pleasure.
From that time my life was different."

—Charles Studd[1]

In human development, as children we are helpless and completely dependent on our parents. We are in awe of the world around us and curious about everything. We love and are loved and trust that our parents will provide for all our needs. We learn the rules and learn that we are rewarded when we obey them and punished when we disobey them. We submit to our parents' will.

Similarly, in the Child stage of faith we discover God and are in awe of Him. We are overwhelmed by His love and overcome by His mercy. We feel joy, demonstrate simple faith, and trust in Him with all our hearts, knowing He will direct our paths (see Proverbs 3:5–6).

---

1. Charles Studd, "I realized that my life," AZ Quotes, accessed Nov. 9, 2022, https://www.azquotes.com/quote/757377.

We are curious and amazed by all we learn about Him and His gospel. We become "as a child, submissive, meek, humble, patient, full of love, willing to submit to all things which the Lord seeth fit to inflict upon [us], even as a child doth submit to his father" (Mosiah 3:19).

At the Child stage of faith, we are truthful, loving, and innocent, and we see only the best in others. We believe that "the Lord God hath power to do all things which are according to his word" (Alma 7:8), and we trust that He will provide for our needs.

SEEKING REDEMPTION

Many who enter this stage later in life approach God seeking relief from pain (e.g., poverty, addiction, divorce, prison, illness, job loss, grief, or loneliness). Some who are steeped in wickedness desperately need a fresh start—a second chance at life—and find redemption through the infinite mercy, love, and grace of Christ.

This sentiment was beautifully penned by John Newton in the lyrics of his hymn "Amazing Grace." Newton was a slave trader who became an abolitionist. Wracked with guilt for his involvement in the slave trade, he found hope and joy in the gospel of Christ. He wrote:

> Amazing grace! How sweet the sound
> That saved a wretch like me!
> I once was lost, but now am found;
> Was blind, but now I see.
>
> 'Twas grace that taught my heart to fear,
> And grace my fears relieved;
> How precious did that grace appear
> The hour I first believed.[2]

---

2. "Amazing Grace Song: The History, Lyrics and Meaning of the iconic song," Connolly Cove, last modified Oct. 6, 2022, https://www.connollycove.com/amazing-grace-song/.

Alma the younger similarly experienced this renewal. He recounted his conversion to his son, Helaman, and explained that he "went about with the sons of Mosiah, seeking to destroy the church of God" (Alma 36:6). An angel appeared to them and commanded them to cease, after which Alma collapsed and was catatonic for three days (see Alma 36:9). He described his experience:

> But I was racked with eternal torment, for my soul was harrowed up to the greatest degree and racked with all my sins.
>
> Yea, I did remember all my sins and iniquities, for which I was tormented with the pains of hell; yea, I saw that I had rebelled against my God, and that I had not kept his holy commandments.
>
> Yea, and I had murdered many of his children, or rather led them away unto destruction; yea, and in fine so great had been my iniquities, that the very thought of coming into the presence of my God did rack my soul with inexpressible horror.
>
> Oh, thought I, that I could be banished and become extinct both soul and body, that I might not be brought to stand in the presence of my God, to be judged of my deeds.
>
> And now, for three days and for three nights was I racked, even with the pains of a damned soul.
>
> And it came to pass that as I was thus racked with torment, while I was harrowed up by the memory of my many sins, behold, I remembered also to have heard my father prophesy unto the people concerning the coming of one Jesus Christ, a Son of God, to atone for the sins of the world.
>
> Now, as my mind caught hold upon this thought, I cried within my heart: O Jesus, thou Son of God, have mercy on me, who am in the gall of bitterness, and am encircled about by the everlasting chains of death.
>
> And now, behold, when I thought this, I could remember my pains no more; yea, I was harrowed up by the memory of my sins no more.
>
> And oh, what joy, and what marvelous light I did behold; yea, my soul was filled with joy as exceeding as was my pain!
>
> Yea, I say unto you, my son, that there could be nothing so exquisite and so bitter as were my pains. Yea, and again I say unto

you, my son, that on the other hand, there can be nothing so exquisite and sweet as was my joy. (Alma 36:12–21)

At the Child stage, we are overwhelmed by God's infinite love, mercy, and grace. We have simple faith that He is all we understand Him to be and that He will do all that He has promised.

SPIRITUAL EXPERIENCES

Some people are converted and enter the Child stage after a significant spiritual experience. Alma's experience with the angel described above is a good example. Saul's vision on the road to Damascus, recorded in Acts 9, is another example. He was "breathing out threatenings and slaughter against the disciples of the Lord" (verse 1) and sought permission from the high priest to go to Damascus to capture the Christians there. On his way, the Lord appeared to him and asked, "Saul, Saul, why persecutest thou me?" (verse 4). Humbled, Saul asked the Lord, "What wilt thou have me to do?" (verse 6).

The Lord told Saul to go into the city where he would receive more instructions. Following that experience, Saul was blind for three days before being healed by Ananias. Then he immediately began preaching in the synagogues that Jesus was the Son of God (see verse 20).

Joseph Smith's experience was even more remarkable. As a four-teen-year-old boy in Manchester, New York, he found that there was "an unusual excitement on the subject of religion" (Joseph Smith— History 1:5) in that region. The fervor of spiritual enthusiasm was coupled with great contention. "For, notwithstanding the great love which the converts to these different faiths expressed at the time of their conversion . . . it was seen that the seemingly good feelings of both the priests and the converts were more pretended than real; for a scene of great confusion and bad feeling ensued—priest contending against priest, and convert against convert; so that all their good feelings one for another, if they ever had any, were entirely lost in a strife of words and a contest about opinions" (Joseph Smith—History 1:6).

The discord and disagreement confused Joseph as he puzzled over which sect he should join. He often asked himself, "Who of all these parties are right; or, are they all wrong together? If any one of them be right, which is it, and how shall I know it?" (Joseph Smith—History 1:10). As he sought for answers to these questions, he read James 1:5: "If any of you lack wisdom, let him ask of God, that giveth to all men liberally, and upbraideth not; and it shall be given him." Joseph explained:

> Never did any passage of scripture come with more power to the heart of man than this did at this time to mine. It seemed to enter with great force into every feeling of my heart. I reflected on it again and again, knowing that if any person needed wisdom from God, I did; for how to act I did not know, and unless I could get more wisdom than I then had, I would never know; for the teachers of religion of the different sects understood the same passages of scripture so differently as to destroy all confidence in settling the question by an appeal to the Bible.
>
> At length I came to the conclusion that I must either remain in darkness and confusion, or else I must do as James directs, that is, ask of God. I at length came to the determination to "ask of God," concluding that if he gave wisdom to them that lacked wisdom, and would give liberally, and not upbraid, I might venture. (Joseph Smith—History 1:12–13)

Then, on a beautiful spring morning in 1820, Joseph entered the woods behind his family's cabin to offer his first prayer. He explained what happened next:

> After I had retired to the place where I had previously designed to go, having looked around me, and finding myself alone, I kneeled down and began to offer up the desires of my heart to God. I had scarcely done so, when immediately I was seized upon by some

power which entirely overcame me, and had such an astonishing influence over me as to bind my tongue so that I could not speak. Thick darkness gathered around me, and it seemed to me for a time as if I were doomed to sudden destruction.

But, exerting all my powers to call upon God to deliver me out of the power of this enemy which had seized upon me, and at the very moment when I was ready to sink into despair and abandon myself to destruction—not to an imaginary ruin, but to the power of some actual being from the unseen world, who had such marvelous power as I had never before felt in any being—just at this moment of great alarm, I saw a pillar of light exactly over my head, above the brightness of the sun, which descended gradually until it fell upon me.

It no sooner appeared than I found myself delivered from the enemy which held me bound. When the light rested upon me I saw two Personages, whose brightness and glory defy all description, standing above me in the air. One of them spake unto me, calling me by name and said, pointing to the other—This is My Beloved Son. Hear Him! (Joseph Smith—History 1:15–17)

The spiritual experiences of Alma, Saul, and Joseph Smith were extraordinary. Most people have spiritual experiences of a lesser magnitude. They are often simple spiritual experiences but have a profound effect on them.

For example, I recently witnessed the conversion of a new member of the Church. I'll call him Mark. Mark had known members of the Church throughout his life, and they had left a positive impression on him. Now, in his seventies, he desired to learn more about the gospel.

A few months ago, he called the mission office and asked if someone could teach him about the Church. The missionaries quickly responded and taught him the first lesson. Among other topics, they taught him to pray and invited him to pray before their next visit. They then scheduled the second lesson and invited me to attend.

At the beginning of the next discussion, the missionaries asked Mark if he had prayed. He then shared a spiritual experience. He explained that he had recently splurged a bit and bought a used BMW. Shortly afterward, he discovered there was a problem with the transfer case, which transfers power from the engine to the front wheels on four-wheel drive vehicles. He called the dealer to ask if he could return the car, and they explained there was no warranty. He then took it to a mechanic, but the cost of the repairs exceeded what he was willing to pay. The mechanic advised him to "just sell the car and be done with it."

He explained that he didn't know what to do. He didn't feel it was ethical to sell the car to someone else knowing it had mechanical problems, but he had to repair it if he was going to keep the car, and the cost of the repairs was too high. He then remembered that the missionaries taught him he could pray to receive answers. So, he offered a humble, sincere prayer. As he prayed about the situation, he felt calm, comforted, and greatly relieved. He knew everything would be well.

After he shared his story, we discussed how God often speaks to us through a feeling of peace. We explained that it is one of the more convincing impressions of the Holy Ghost.

This simple answer to a heartfelt prayer was, for Mark, a powerful spiritual experience that precipitated his conversion. Shortly thereafter, he was baptized, and as promised, everything worked out. Someone recommended another mechanic who was able to repair it for much less.

Later, Mark recalled the experience. He said he was in awe that God knew who he was, was aware of his needs, responded to a relatively trivial circumstance, comforted him to relieve his distress, and helped him find a solution. This sense of awe is a hallmark of the Child stage of faith.

Spiritual experiences like these lead some into the Child stage of faith. Others enter the Child stage without a significant spiritual experience. They simply believe in God and the restoration of the gospel, and that is enough for them to enter the Child stage.

OBEDIENCE

At the Child stage, we are also committed to serve God and follow Christ. Our commitment is demonstrated through obedience. For this reason, obedience is a preeminent principle for children in Primary. They learn this principle from many of the songs they sing. For example.

- "Keep the commandments . . . He will send blessings."[3]
- "I will go and do the thing the Lord commands. I know the Lord provides a way; he wants me to obey."[4]
- "We have been taught and we understand, that we must do as the Lord commands."[5]

At the Child stage, scriptures about obedience resonate with us.

- "If ye love me, keep my commandments" (John 14:15).
- "To obey is better than sacrifice" (I Samuel 15:22).
- "Not every one that saith unto me, Lord, Lord, shall enter into the kingdom of heaven; but he that doeth the will of my Father which is in heaven" (Matthew 7:21).
- "There is a law, irrevocably decreed in heaven before the foundations of this world, upon which all blessings are predicated—And when we obtain any blessing from God,

---

3. "Keep the Commandments," Children's Songbook, 146–47.
4. "Nephi's Courage," Children's Songbook, 120–21.
5. "We'll Bring the World His Truth (Army of Helaman)," Children's Songbook, 172–73.

it is by obedience to that law upon which it is predicated" (Doctrine and Covenants 130: 20–21)

At the Child stage, obedience is often motivated by our hope for blessings or our fear of punishment. We may create a transactional relationship with God and do His will in exchange for His blessings or to allay His punishments.[6] After all, He did say "I, the Lord, am bound when ye do what I say; but when ye do not what I say, ye have no promise" (Doctrine and Covenants 82:10).

At best, this hope for promised blessings gives us cause to believe and leads us to do good, strengthening our faith. At worst, it causes us to become superstitious and believe that all good that comes into our life is the result of obedience to the commandments, and all evil is the result of disobedience. Though this may be true at times, there are also times when things happen in the course of life that may not directly correlate to our obedience. The Savior explained that His Father "maketh his sun to rise on the evil and on the good, and sendeth rain on the just and on the unjust" (Matthew 5:45).

STAGNATION AT THE CHILD STAGE

When we stagnate at the Child stage, our spiritual growth slows, and we become painfully aware of our unworthiness. At this stage, we practice our faith through obedience but may find ourselves slipping back into old habits and returning to our favorite sins "like the dog to his vomit, or like the sow to her wallowing in the mire" (3 Nephi 7:8). We convince ourselves that the spiritual giants we admire live blissfully free from sin, forgetting that "all have sinned, and come short of the glory of God" (Romans 3:23). We feel guilt and shame, and we fear that our quest to be perfected in Christ is hopeless because

---

6. See Janet O. Hagberg and Robert A. Guelich, *The Critical Journey: Stages in the Life of Faith* (Salem, WI: Sheffield Publishing Company, 2005), 45.

we cannot deny all ungodliness (see Moroni 10:32) and know that "the Lord cannot look upon sin with the least degree of allowance" (Doctrine and Covenants 1:31).

We also become aware of our lack of knowledge and understanding. The more we learn, the more we become aware of all that we have yet to learn. Our ignorance is a threat to our salvation, for "it is impossible for a man to be saved in ignorance" (Doctrine and Covenants 131:6). Those around us appear to have a much deeper understanding of the doctrines, can quote the prophets, have a firm grasp of the scriptures, and can explain the cultural and historical backgrounds to give context to the ideas, while we're still not sure if the book of Jarom is in the Book of Mormon or the Old Testament. Our childlike faith, submissiveness, and meekness seem like weaknesses when measured against their spiritual superpowers.

Crisis at the Child Stage

The winter of faith at the Child stage stems from feelings of inadequacy and worthlessness—a spiritual bankruptcy. Janet Hagberg and Robert Guelich explained in their book, *The Critical Journey*, that we feel "there is nothing there; no well to draw from; no energy left. We feel that no one cares for us, certainly not God, because if God really cared, we would be rescued. We look for miracles but know they will never occur for us. We do not deserve them. We feel we have nowhere to turn and even God is not listening."[7]

Transition from Child to Adolescent

This feeling of inadequacy associated with this winter of faith can trigger our transition from the Child stage to the Adolescent stage.

---

7. Hagberg and Guelich, *The Critical Journey*, 44.

We become increasingly aware we don't measure up to our peers in our faith community and that we need to grow up. We feel a desire to fit in (Social) and see there are things we need to change to do so.

ENDURING THE CRISIS

Most of us endure the crisis at the Child stage. Over time, through personal study and church attendance, we develop a deeper understanding of the doctrines and knowledge of the gospel. We begin to understand that perfection is more a process than a destination, and we put less pressure on ourselves to be perfect. We also sense our heavenly parents' loving patience and support as we stumble and fall on our path to perfection. We develop friendships in church and become valued members of the community as we serve others and magnify our callings, satisfying our Social needs.

KEY POINT SUMMARY

- In the Child stage, we are in awe of God's infinite love, mercy, grace, and power.
- Spiritual experiences or a desire for redemption may lead us into the Child stage.
- Obedience is an important characteristic of the Child stage.
- Crisis in the Child stage often results from feelings of inadequacy and worthlessness.

4

THE ADOLESCENT
STAGE OF FAITH

"This is a divine work in process, with the manifestations and blessings of it abounding in every direction, so please don't hyperventilate if from time to time issues arise that need to be examined, understood, and resolved. They do and they will. In this Church, what we know will always trump what we do not know. And remember, in this world, everyone is to walk by faith."

—Elder Jeffrey R. Holland[1]

In human development, as we enter adolescence, we instinctively push against our parents and seek independence, an important step to becoming an adult. As we push away from our parents, we subconsciously know that we are also pushing away from our only safe and sure social group (assuming we have a loving family). We then instinctively form bonds with another social group so we can again feel safe and secure outside of family bonds. Therefore, fitting into our friend group becomes paramount, and our parents' counsel, rules, and

1. Jeffrey R. Holland, "'Lord, I Believe,'" *Ensign* or *Liahona*, May 2013, 94.

expectations become less so. We quickly learn the social norms—the informal, unwritten rules—for the group, and we conform to those norms. They may include our dress, music we listen to, movies we watch, language we use, food we eat, and rules we break. We discover the norms by watching what others do and mimicking them. We also learn they may ridicule or ostracize us when we do something that does not fit the norm. Gradually, we learn the norms and modify our behaviors to fit in.

As children, we learn that our parents favor us when we are obedient to the formal rules. As adolescents, we discount obedience to formal rules and favor conformity to our social group's norms.

The Adolescent stage of faith is similar to the adolescent stage of human development. Our driving desire is to fit into the social group—the Church. We want to belong, to be included, and to satisfy our Social needs on Maslow's hierarchy.

The Adolescent stage is an important stage in our spiritual development. There are three types of conversion: social, intellectual, and spiritual. The strongest members of the Church are those who have experienced all three. Social conversion normally occurs at the Adolescent stage.

CULTURAL NORMS

Since social acceptance depends largely on conformity to social norms, at the Adolescent stage we become very aware of the Church's cultural norms and strive to conform to them. Most of the Church's norms are requisite for eternal salvation and establish a culture consistent with the doctrine of Christ. Service, charity, sacrifice, unity, worship, reverence, and order are all examples of Church norms. Each of these are important characteristics of the Church and create a

Christian culture. We do well to conform to these norms and encourage others to conform to them as well.

However, in the Church, as in all communities, there are other norms that are not essential for salvation. We have adopted many such norms since the Church was established in 1830. Here are a few examples of modern norms you may be familiar with.

- Priesthood holders should wear white shirts when administering the sacrament.
- Members should not drink caffeinated beverages.
- Priesthood leaders should not have facial hair.
- Women should wear no more than one earring in each ear.
- We fold our arms when we pray.
- We should not play card games with "face" cards.
- We should not watch TV on Sundays.
- We should not get tattoos.

Many norms like these can be traced back to the teachings of modern-day prophets and apostles who established these norms with good intent. It should be noted that these norms are not commandments. They are given "not by commandment or constraint, but by revelation and the word of wisdom" (Doctrine and Covenants 89:2). But when we are in the Adolescent stage of faith, we may fixate on norms like these and become like the Pharisees. Once, the Pharisees were complaining to Jesus that His disciples were not keeping "the tradition of the elders" (Mark 7:3); they were not doing some of the ritualistic washing that the Pharisees required. Jesus reprimanded the Pharisees and called them hypocrites (see Mark 7:6). He described them by saying:

> Howbeit in vain do they worship me, teaching for doctrines the commandments of men.

> For laying aside the commandment of God, ye hold the tradition of men, as the washing of pots and cups: and many other such like things ye do.
>
> And he said unto them, Full well ye reject the commandment of God, that ye may keep your own tradition. (Mark 7:7–9)

At the Adolescent stage, the cultural norms and traditions may take precedence over obedience to the commandments. The Pharisees are a good example. They were spiritually stuck at the Adolescent stage.

When I was serving as a missionary in Harrisburg, Illinois, my companion and I were visiting with a family we were teaching. The husband mentioned he had a leak in his roof and would be working on it that weekend. Following Ammon's example of service (see Alma 17:25), we offered to help. He replied, "That would be great! Come over on Sunday afternoon. We can work on it then."

My companion and I agreed to come back on Sunday to help, but I was visibly concerned as we walked to our car after the visit. My companion noticed and asked what was wrong. I explained, "We agreed to work on his house on Sunday, the Sabbath. We aren't supposed to work on the Sabbath." As I was speaking, I was remembering the words of the Lord recorded in Exodus 20:

> Remember the sabbath day, to keep it holy.
>
> Six days shalt thou labour, and do all thy work:
>
> But the seventh day is the sabbath of the Lord thy God: in it thou shalt not do any work, thou, nor thy son, nor thy daughter, thy manservant, nor thy maidservant, nor thy cattle, nor thy stranger that is within thy gates:
>
> For in six days the Lord made heaven and earth, the sea, and all that in them is, and rested the seventh day: wherefore the Lord blessed the sabbath day, and hallowed it. (verses 8–11)

My companion rolled his eyes at me and said matter-of-factly, "It's okay to serve on the Sabbath."

He was teaching me what Jesus taught the Pharisees. One day, Jesus came upon a man who had a withered hand. It was the Sabbath, and the Pharisees had already had an altercation with Jesus and His disciples earlier that day regarding proper Sabbath observance (see Matthew 12:1–8). The Pharisees, wanting to catch Jesus in His words, asked if it was lawful to heal on the Sabbath. Work was forbidden on the Sabbath, and healing someone could be considered work. Jesus asked which of them, if one of their sheep fell in a pit on the Sabbath, would not lift it out. He then explained that people are more important than sheep and stated, "It is lawful to do well on the sabbath days" (see Matthew 12:12). Then He healed the man's hand.

I was at the Adolescent stage of faith and was blinded by my commitment to Sabbath cultural norms. My companion had to remind me that it was "lawful to do well on the sabbath days" (Matthew 12:12).

Quest for Knowledge

Another characteristic of the Adolescent stage is a quest for knowledge. At the transition point from the Child stage, we become uncomfortably aware of how little we know. Our desire to increase our knowledge can motivate us to move to the Adolescent stage. At this stage, we recognize that "if a person gains more knowledge and intelligence in this life through his diligence and obedience than another, he will have so much the advantage in the world to come" (Doctrine and Covenants 130:19). Many at this stage "feast upon the words of Christ" (2 Nephi 32:3) and seek "out of the best books words of wisdom, [and] seek learning even by study and also by faith" (Doctrine and Covenants 109:7).

We can experience tremendous spiritual growth in the Adolescent stage. Our quest for knowledge nourishes the seed of our faith, and as our knowledge increases, so does our faith and testimony. We become more confident members of the Church. We fit in and feel like we belong. The Church feels like our family.

Respect for Authority

At the Adolescent stage, we have great respect for Joseph Smith, Brigham Young, and the other founding prophets and apostles. We also have great respect for modern-day prophets and apostles, stake presidents, bishops, teachers, and other positive influences in the Church. We trust them. We look to them for counsel and guidance. We study their teachings and listen intently to them when they speak. We commit ourselves to their mission and align our activities with their vision.

Missionary Zeal

At this stage, we feel enlightened and are anxious to share with others what we have discovered. When we do, we may feel confused or disappointed when others are not moved like we are when they hear the messages of prophets and apostles, read the Book of Mormon, or attend church meetings.

Stagnation at the Adolescent Stage

When we become stagnant at the Adolescent stage, we can develop an "us versus them" mindset. At the Child stage, we believe we are wrong and weak and that others in the Church are right and strong. At the Adolescent stage, we believe we are right and strong and others are wrong and weak.[2]

---

2. See Janet O. Hagberg and Robert A. Guelich, *The Critical Journey: Stages in the Life of Faith* (Salem, WI: Sheffield Publishing Company, 2005), 64.

We can become rigid and judgmental of those who do not conform to the cultural norms. Like the Pharisees, we teach "for doctrines the commandments of men" (Mark 7:7). We may think less of another Latter-day Saint who mentions watching TV on Sunday or a young woman who has multiple earrings. At worst, we may smell alcohol or marijuana on the person next to us in the pew at Sacrament Meeting. We may wrinkle our nose and look sideways at them as if they do not belong, forgetting that "they that are whole have no need of the physician" (Mark 2:17) and that The Church of Jesus Christ of Latter-day Saints is not a sanctuary for saints; it is a "hospital for sinners."[3]

At this stage, we are blind to our closed-mindedness and rigidity because we are convinced we are right. And what is right for us is right for all. Our quest for knowledge makes us prideful, for "knowledge puffeth up" (1 Corinthians 8:1). We have found "the way" (John 14:6). We are less troubled by doubts and fears because we now have all the answers and a community that supports us.

The evidence we collect through our study assures us that The Church of Jesus Christ of Latter-day Saints is "the only true and living church upon the face of the whole earth" (Doctrine and Covenants 1:30). But when we are stagnant at the Adolescent stage, we may forget that "much that is inspiring, noble, and worthy of the highest respect is found in many other faiths,"[4] and that other Christian sects profess most of the gospel truths that are essential for salvation.

Crisis at the Adolescent Stage

A winter of faith at the Adolescent stage can occur when our certainty is shaken by uncertainty, which threatens our need for security

---

3. Dale G. Renlund, "Lifelong Conversion" (Brigham Young University devotional, Sept. 14, 2021), 4, speeches.byu.edu.

4. *General Handbook: Serving in The Church of Jesus Christ of Latter-day Saints*, 38.8.29, ChurchofJesusChrist.org.

(the Safety need). Perhaps there is a question for which we cannot find a satisfactory answer.

Tom Phillips served as a bishop, stake president, area executive secretary, the area controller for the British Isles and Africa, and the financial director for the Church's UK corporate entities. As he was preparing to serve as a mission president, he experienced a crisis of faith that stemmed from an unanswered question. He questioned the scriptures in the Book of Mormon that asserted there was no death prior to the fall (see Alma 12:23–24; 2 Nephi 2:22). It was a question he had answered for others many times before, but he had never felt satisfied with the answer—it did not square with the science. He then set out to prove the flaw in the science so he could answer this question for the missionaries and those they taught. He explained:

> Not for one minute, at that time, did I think the Church was false. *I knew*, beyond any shadow of doubt, it was true. I just needed to know what was wrong with the currently held scientific views. After studying the specific scientific methodology, to my amazement, it stood up. These were not simply hypotheses and theories of scientists but demonstrable *facts*. I believed God to be the "Master Scientist." How else can He be the creator of all things? Therefore, true science cannot be in conflict with His revealed word.
>
> This led me to consider in more depth other truth claims of the Church and discuss them with two general authorities and consult two Brigham Young University professors. Conclusion: The Church was not true and I allowed myself to be deceived.[5]

For some of us, as with Tom, a crisis of faith can stem from unanswered questions. Some of us also experience a crisis of faith when there is a change in leadership, direction, or Church policy. We become disillusioned with the Church because we were certain all was

---

5. Tom Phillips, "My Second Anointing Experience," MormonThink, accessed Nov. 10, 2022, http://www.mormonthink.com/personalstories/tomphillips.htm.

right, but now what was right is changing. We conclude either the change is wrong or the Church was wrong all along, because surely *we* are *not* wrong. Joseph Smith once said:

> I have tried for a number of years to get the minds of the Saints prepared to receive the things of God; but we frequently see some of them, after suffering all they have for the work of God, will fly to pieces like glass as soon as anything comes that is contrary to their traditions: they cannot stand the fire at all. How many will be able to abide a celestial law, and go through and receive their exaltation, I am unable to say, as many are called, but few are chosen.[6]

One example of this was when the First Presidency declared that all worthy males could receive the priesthood. While most Latter-day Saints saw this change in policy as a long-awaited blessing, others believed this was "the final step in the Church's apostasy."[7] There were similar dissenters when the Church discontinued polygamy.[8] More recently, many experienced a crisis of faith when the Church announced its restrictive LGBTQ policies in 2015. Ostler's survey of members of the Church who were experiencing a crisis of faith revealed that 99% said that those policies contributed to their crisis of faith.[9]

When we are children, we believe our parents have all the answers. When we become adolescents, we learn a few things in school and online and are convinced that we are the experts and our parents are foolish. Mark Twain once said, "When I was a boy of fourteen, my father was so ignorant I could hardly stand to have the old man

---

6. *Teachings of Presidents of the Church: Joseph Smith* (2007), 520.

7. Chad J. Flake, "Mormon Bibliography 1978," *BYU Studies* 20, no. 1 (Fall 1979): 112.

8. See *Gospel Topics Essays*, "The Manifesto and the End of Plural Marriage," ChurchofJesusChrist.org.

9. See David B. Ostler, *Bridges: Ministering to Those Who Question* (Salt Lake City: Greg Kofford Books, 2019), 31.

around. But when I got to twenty-one, I was astonished at how much the old man had learned in seven years."[10]

Similarly, at the Child stage of faith, we are in awe of all there is to learn in the Church about the gospel of Jesus Christ. We see that the Church has all the answers. At the Adolescent stage, we learn a few things as we "feast upon the words of Christ" (2 Nephi 32:3) and come to believe we are experts in our own right. Then we learn something we didn't know or is difficult to believe and it seems like foolishness to us. We may experience a winter of faith as we discover that our understanding of doctrine conflicts with official Church doctrine or the opinion of a respected leader.

For example, many experienced a winter of faith when the Church posted the Gospel Topics Essays on its website. The intent of the essays was to provide "accurate information" to counter the misinformation so prevalent from "questionable and inaccurate sources." [11] While the essays clarified many points, they also confirmed some of the criticisms levied at the Church. Examples of these include Joseph Smith translating the Book of Mormon by putting seer stones in a hat and pressing his face into the hat[12] and the fact that he practiced polygamy and married a 14-year-old girl.[13]

Many had heard these claims from critics of the Church and disregarded them, only to learn from the essays that they were true. They felt duped. They believed the Church had deceitfully concealed these things and now confessed them only because it was caught in deceit. Ostler's survey of members of the Church that were experiencing a

---

10. "Bringing Up Father," *Reader's Digest* 31, no. 9 (Sept. 1937): 22.

11. *Gospel Topics Essays*, ChurchofJesusChrist.org.

12. See *Gospel Topics Essays*, "Book of Mormon Translation," ChurchofJesusChrist.org.

13. See *Gospel Topics Essays*, "Plural Marriage in Kirtland and Nauvoo," ChurchofJesusChrist.org.

crisis of faith revealed that 100% of the respondents said that concerns with Church history contributed to their crisis of faith. One respondent commented, "I have a hard time trusting the Church because of the many times I was lied to about Church history."[14] Countless Latter-day Saints experienced a cold winter of faith and many entered the dark night of the soul after reading the Gospel Topics Essays.

Experiences like these teach us that we don't know what we don't know. At the Adolescent stage, we convince ourselves that we know all we need to know and then are shaken when we learn what we *don't* know.

Our disillusionment with the Church can cause us to feel betrayed, certain that we have kept the faith while others have not. One anonymous member described his experience: "I felt an incredible sense of betrayal. Especially when I was expected to 'be honest in my dealings with my fellow man,' when the very organization asking me at my temple recommend interview was not honest in its correlated doctrinal and historical teachings. . . . Nothing can restore my faith in the LDS Church. The evidence is clear that they are engaged in a pattern of deception and fraud to continually mislead their own members and the public."[15]

We may share our concerns with our leaders, only to have them dismiss those concerns. At worst, we approach them humbly seeking answers and they reject us. Ostler shared this example:

> I want to tell you about Allison, who is in her late thirties and holds a temple recommend. She and her husband are raising two teenage daughters. While she was teaching Church History and the Doctrine and Covenants to teenagers in early-morning seminary, she had questions that led her to studying parts of the Church's early

---

14. Ostler, *Bridges*, 29.

15. *LDS Personal Faith Crisis*, PDF file, June 2013, https://faenrandir.github. io/a_careful_examination/documents/faith_crisis_study/Faith_Crisis_ R28e.pdf.

history that challenged her faith. Then, while serving as the Primary president in her ward, she found herself struggling with her belief and wanted help in figuring out how to continue participating in church despite her questions. She felt alone and wanted to discuss her concerns with someone. She didn't feel comfortable going to her bishop, who had earlier dismissed her attempts to introduce the Gospel Topics Essays to ward members and referred to them as "anti-Mormon materials."

She went to the stake president, who strongly encouraged her to talk with her bishop. With some trepidation that doing so would affect her standing in the ward, she and her husband sat down with her bishop. Allison expressed that she "had concerns but was really committed to staying in the Church." She explained that in Young Women, her daughter had discussed how Joseph Smith used a seer stone to help translate the Book of Mormon. Her teacher strongly rebuked her and later told Allison to be more careful in deciding what materials to let her daughter read. The bishop was surprised that Allison had concerns since she appeared to be a completely believing member.

After the meeting, Allison and her husband felt good about both being able to honestly express their concerns and that their bishop had listened to them. However, two or three weeks later, the bishop released both Allison and her husband from their callings without explanation. Allison expressed to her bishop that this was a real setback and that she didn't know how she would participate in church moving forward. Shortly thereafter, a friend of Allison's in the Primary presidency submitted her name to the bishop for approval to call her as a teacher in the Primary. The bishop turned down the sister, telling her that Allison was not worthy.

Allison and her family don't know what to do next. Their oldest daughter is planning on serving a mission, but Allison now feels unwelcome in her ward and has lost trust in her bishop. She and her husband haven't held callings for six months and haven't been invited to participate in any way. They plan to move soon and won't be opening up about their concerns in their next ward.[16]

---

16. Ostler, *Bridges*, 77–78.

From the outside looking in, it is easy to criticize the actions of Allison's bishop. However, after serving as a bishop twice, I now realize how ill-equipped I was to support those suffering a crisis of faith and feel some sympathy for him. Certainly, he responded with the best intentions. Perhaps he felt he needed to protect the children and youth from what he believed was misinformation, and releasing her and her husband was the most expedient solution. Regardless, he probably would have responded differently if he had a deeper understanding of the complexities of faith. As I consider those I counseled in crisis, I wish I had then the knowledge and wisdom that I have now. I would have listened more, loved them more, shown more patience, and given them better counsel. Perhaps Allison's bishop will one day look back on his experience with Allison and feel similar regret.

If our leaders reject us, the Church, which was our safe place, now feels threatening, and we may begin to look elsewhere for security. Perhaps we attend another ward outside of our boundaries or move to a different stake. We may attend churches of other faiths or search for respite in nonreligious groups or literature that offer alternative forms of spirituality. Though our quest for truth is sincere, we are not progressing on our journey. Our movement merely creates the illusion of progress.

Ironically, the knowledge we initially pursued to better fit into our Church community can eventually become the wedge that causes us to consider leaving it. Nephi's brother, Jacob, reminds us that our knowledge, if left unchecked, can deceive us: "O that cunning plan of the evil one! O the vainness, and the frailties, and the foolishness of men! When they are learned they think they are wise, and they hearken not unto the counsel of God, for they set it aside, supposing they know of themselves, wherefore, their wisdom is foolishness and it profiteth them not. And they shall perish" (2 Nephi 9:28).

Transitioning from Adolescent to Young Adult

If we are stagnant at the Adolescent stage, transition to the Young Adult stage is unlikely. We should first stop "looking beyond the mark" (Jacob 4:14) and return to the plain and simple truths of the gospel. We should remember that "to be learned is good *if* [we] hearken unto the counsels of God" (2 Nephi 9:29; emphasis added). This may require us to step back into the Child stage and rediscover God's love for us and our awe of His infinite grace.

Enduring the Crisis

Dieter F. Uchtdorf, who was then the Second Counselor in the First Presidency, spoke to those in the Adolescent stage of faith when he spoke in general conference:

> First doubt your doubts before you doubt your faith. We must never allow doubt to hold us prisoner and keep us from the divine love, peace, and gifts that come through faith in the Lord Jesus Christ.
>
> Some might say, "I just don't fit in with you people in the Church."
>
> If you could see into our hearts, you would probably find that you fit in better than you suppose. You might be surprised to find that we have yearnings and struggles and hopes similar to yours. Your background or upbringing might seem different from what you perceive in many Latter-day Saints, but that could be a blessing. Brothers and sisters, dear friends, we need your unique talents and perspectives. The diversity of persons and peoples all around the globe is a strength of this Church.
>
> Some might say, "I don't think I could live up to your standards."
>
> All the more reason to come! The Church is designed to nourish the imperfect, the struggling, and the exhausted. It is filled with people who desire with all their heart to keep the commandments, even if they haven't mastered them yet.

Some might say, "I know a member of your Church who is a hypocrite. I could never join a church that had someone like him as a member."

If you define a hypocrite as someone who fails to live up perfectly to what he or she believes, then we are all hypocrites. None of us is quite as Christlike as we know we should be. But we earnestly desire to overcome our faults and the tendency to sin. With our heart and soul we yearn to become better with the help of the Atonement of Jesus Christ.

If these are your desires, then regardless of your circumstances, your personal history, or the strength of your testimony, there is room for you in this Church. Come, join with us![17]

As we transition from the Adolescent stage, we learn to "trust in the Lord with all [our] heart; and lean not unto [our] own understanding" (Proverbs 3:5). We begin to comprehend that, despite all we have learned, there is still much to learn and that the Lord will teach us "line upon line, precept upon precept, here a little and there a little" (2 Nephi 28:30). He assures us that if we continue to listen and obey, we will continue to "learn wisdom" (verse 30). He promises that "unto him that receiveth I will give more" and warns that those who say "we have enough, from them shall be taken away even that which they have" (verse 30).

We acknowledge that there may be some principles, doctrines, or events in Church history that we cannot yet accept, understand, or explain. We remember that the Lord taught, "My thoughts are not your thoughts, neither are your ways my ways . . . For as the heavens are higher than the earth, so are my ways higher than your ways, and my thoughts than your thoughts" (Isaiah 55: 8–9). We are willing to temporarily set aside our concerns until we are ready to receive greater light and knowledge. We remember that the Jews of Old Testament

---

17. Dieter F. Uchtdorf, "Come, Join with Us," *Ensign* or *Liahona*, Nov. 2013, 23.

times "were a stiffnecked people; and they despised the words of plainness" (Jacob 4:14). They also "sought for things that they could not understand" and became blinded "by looking beyond the mark" (verse 14). As a result, God took "away his plainness from them, and delivered unto them many things which they [could not] understand, because they desired it" (verse 14). Eventually, they "stumbled" and rejected their Messiah (see verse 15).

We also begin to understand that The Church of Jesus Christ of Latter-day Saints is a perfect church of imperfect people. We accept that the Church is true, though its members are sometimes untrue to themselves and to the Lord. We become less judgmental of those who do not conform to cultural norms and are more forgiving and supportive of those who break the commandments.

Once we are satisfied that we belong in the Church and fit into the community (Social), we become more concerned about making a difference. Our desires transition from Social needs to Esteem needs. This desire leads us to the Young Adult stage of faith.

Key Point Summary

- The hallmark of the Adolescent stage is fitting into the Church community.
- Some prioritize cultural norms over gospel principles.
- Crises of faith occur when certainty is shaken.

5

THE YOUNG ADULT
STAGE OF FAITH

*"I will have nothing to do with a God who cares only occasionally.
I need a God who is with us always, everywhere, in the deepest
depths as well as the highest heights. It is when things go wrong,
when good things do not happen, when our prayers seem to have
been lost, that God is most present. We do not need the sheltering
wings when things go smoothly. We are closest to God
in the darkness, stumbling along blindly."*

—Madeleine L'Engle[1]

In human development, many young adults go to college or learn a trade and start their careers. They are ambitious, have big dreams, and want to make their mark on the world. They are determined to be successful, respected, and admired and work hard to that end.

Others on similar paths are humbler. Their need for Esteem is satisfied when they are appreciated—when they feel like they don't

---

1. Madeleine L'Engle, "I will have nothing," AZ Quotes, accessed Nov. 9, 2022, https://www.azquotes.com/quote/355599.

just *belong* in their teams and social groups but are truly *needed.* They want to be valued for their skills and talents and contribute meaningfully to the organizations they choose and the world at large.

Similarly, in the Young Adult stage of faith, our desire for Esteem motivates us to serve God. We readily accept assignments and callings and serve the Lord "with full purpose of heart, and . . . with all diligence of mind" (Mosiah 7:33). Hagberg and Guelich described this stage as "positive and dynamic, centered on being productive in the area of our faith. It nourishes us because it is so personally rewarding, even when the objective is to help others. In helping or leading, we also are fed, so it operates on goals and achievements, building and creating."[2]

We are very productive in the Young Adult stage, for we know that "not every one that saith unto me, Lord, Lord, shall enter into the kingdom of heaven; but he that doeth the will of my Father which is in heaven" (Matthew 7:21). We subscribe to James' lecture on faith and demonstrate our faith through works:

> Even so faith, if it hath not works, is dead, being alone.
>
> Yea, a man may say, Thou hast faith, and I have works: shew me thy faith without thy works, and I will shew thee my faith by my works.
>
> But wilt thou know, O vain man, that faith without works is dead?
>
> Ye see then how that by works a man is justified, and not by faith only. (James 2:17–20, 24)

During this stage, we love to set and achieve goals. We create and celebrate church programs that have measurable outcomes. We acknowledge that the members of the church are "numbered" (Moroni 6:4), and we recognize that our joy will be great with one soul that we

---

2. Janet O. Hagberg and Robert A. Guelich, *The Critical Journey: Stages in the Life of Faith* (Salem, WI: Sheffield Publishing Company, 2005), 73.

bring into the Church and even greater if we should bring many souls (see Doctrine and Covenants 18:16).

The Young Adult stage is the most energizing and rewarding stage of faith and can feel like the pinnacle of our spiritual experience. Hagberg and Guelig explained that the Young Adult stage is "the height of [our] faith experience. It feels exciting, fulfilling, awesome, inspiring, fruitful."[3] We accomplish much that is good as we enthusiastically serve others and build the kingdom of God. We feel like we are contributing, valued, and accomplished, which satisfies our Esteem need. Since we have not experienced a higher stage of faith, we may suppose we are at the highest stage of spiritual development. For this reason, it is common for the Young Adult stage to become a home stage.

CHURCH FITS US

During the Child stage, we want the Church to be right. At the Adolescent stage, we want to be right. At the Young Adult stage, we want the Church to be right for us. In human development, as adolescents become young adults, they look less for groups they will fit in with and more for groups that fit them. Adolescence is largely about discovering identity. As people emerge from adolescence and become young adults, they have a more defined sense of who they are and choose schools, organizations, peer groups, and causes that fit the person they have become and will shape them into who they plan to be. Similarly, in the Young Adult stage of faith, we become less concerned about fitting in with the Church and more concerned about the Church fitting us.

---

3. Hagberg and Guelich, *The Critical Journey*, 74.

Equality

As we transition out of the Adolescent stage, we successfully navigate around those points of doctrine or Church history that conflict with our views and values. At the Young Adult stage, we begin to appreciate the nuances in the Church and are better able to discern between doctrine and tradition, cultural norm and commandment. We are more aware of the flaws in our faith, acknowledge the contradictions in our tradition, and are more accepting of other religions and worldviews. Thomas McConkie explained that at this stage, "we develop a great capacity to recognize the interiors of others. Our shared humanity is a more steady presence in awareness. We start to clearly discern the dignity of all humans and advocate for equality in all aspects of civic life."[4]

As we are more prone to advocate for equality at this stage, we become acutely aware of marginalized members of our community. For example, gender roles in the Church have become a pressing concern for many. Of those Ostler surveyed, 99% said that gender roles contributed to their crises of faith. One female respondent said, "Our experience is much like our mothers'. We are told we are equal and powerful and relevant, except that we aren't. We hold no power, no real decision-making. We are presided over in every aspect of the gospel. It's suffocating and disempowering."[5]

Buffet Religion

At the Young Adult stage, we also become better at determining "the weightier matters of the law, judgment, mercy, and faith"

---

4. Thomas Wirthlin McConkie, *Navigating the Mormon Faith Crisis: A Simple Development Map* (Salt Lake City: Mormon Stages, 2015), 95.

5. David B. Ostler, *Bridges: Ministering to Those Who Question* (Salt Lake City: Greg Kofford Books, 2019), 33.

(Matthew 23:23). We prioritize certain aspects of the Church and choose what we believe is essential for our salvation. This appears to some as "buffet religion" but is an important step in our spiritual development. Choosing what is right for us in the Church allows us to be flexible in the face of uncertainty and makes us more resilient to doubt. Thomas McConkie noted, "Life at [the Young Adult stage] is complex; black and white answers feel too simplistic. There is legitimate doubt to contend with here. . . . Moreover, the [Young Adult] knows that when engaged with honestly, doubt can lead to more mature expressions of faith."[6]

> *Doubt can lead to more mature expressions of faith.*

ESTEEM

Some of us are humble and "magnify our office" (Jacob 1:19) "with an eye single to the glory of God" (Doctrine and Covenants 4:5), while others of us "aspire to the honors of men" (Doctrine and Covenants 121:35) and undertake "to gratify our pride [and] vain ambition" (Doctrine and Covenants 121:37). Some prefer to be in the spotlight and some prefer to shine the spotlight on others. Regardless of which side of the spotlight we are on, we are motivated by a desire to be valued and esteemed in the Church community. Our need for Esteem is a great motivator, but unfortunately it is a poor navigator.[7] It can motivate us to do much good and can lead us to do much evil.

In the Young Adult stage, we recognize our spiritual gifts and leverage those to accomplish the work of the Lord. We also like when others see our gifts, and we bask in their praise. We may convince

---

6. McConkie, *Navigating the Mormon Faith Crisis,* 100.

7. See David Marcum and Steven Smith, *egonomics: What Makes Ego Our Greatest Asset (or Most Expensive Liability)* (New York City: Touchstone, 2008).

ourselves that our gifts make us indispensable and that no one else could do what we do as well as we do it. Naturally, we feel like we should be selected for certain assignments and callings and may feel offended if not chosen. We forget that "there are many called, but few are chosen. And why are they not chosen? Because their hearts are set so much upon the things of this world, and aspire to the honors of men" (Doctrine and Covenants 121:34–35).

ANXIOUSLY ENGAGED

At this stage, we are good and faithful servants who love to be busy. We are "anxiously engaged in a good cause, and do many things of [our] own free will, and bring to pass much righteousness" (Doctrine and Covenants 58:27). And as we continue to "do good," we "shall in nowise lose [our] reward" (Doctrine and Covenants 58:28). I'm sure the Lord smiles on some of us in loving, patient amusement as we "waste and wear out our lives" (Doctrine and Covenants 123:13) purporting to build His kingdom, while He knows that in our hearts we are eager to build our own. We may supplant God's desires with our own while declaring, "God's will be done!" Despite appearances, some of us are more self-serving than serving.

TEACHABILITY

We may believe we are more mentor than mentee and that we "are not sent forth to be taught, but to teach" (Doctrine and Covenants 43:15). The success we experience during this stage, coupled with the knowledge we gained at the Adolescent stage, leads us to believe we are wiser than we are. We may gracefully decline mentoring from others or furrow our brows at counsel from our bishop, stake president, or prophet as we measure their inspiration against our wisdom.

FACADE OF PERFECTION

At the Young Adult stage, "life becomes a performance."[8] We cannot appear vulnerable or weak in front of others, so we maintain a facade of perfection. Those around us admire our faithfulness, diligence, and obedience. All the while, we fear they will see who we really are. We fear they will see our frustration, weakness, fears, tears, discouragement, or depression. We fear they will discover our sins and see that we are less like the Savior and more like the scribes and Pharisees, hypocrites who are "whited sepulchres, which indeed appear beautiful outward, but are within full . . . of all uncleanness" (Matthew 23:27). And though we "outwardly appear righteous unto men . . . within [we] are full of hypocrisy and iniquity" (Matthew 23:28). As we strive to "be perfect even as [Christ], or [our] Father who is in heaven is perfect" (3 Nephi 12:48), we become acutely and painfully aware of how imperfect we are.

STAGNATION AT THE YOUNG ADULT STAGE

Since we may believe the Young Adult Stage is the pinnacle of our spiritual development, it is common for us to stagnate at this stage. When we stagnate at the Young Adult stage, we burn out. We become "weary in well doing" (Galatians 6:9), having forgotten "that all these things [should be] done in wisdom and order; for it is not requisite that a man should run faster than he has strength" (Mosiah 4:27). Because our identity has become more wrapped up in what we *do* than who we *are,*[9] we may lose sight of ourselves. We may feel unappreciated and may not know why. We may blame others for our shortfalls, failures, or doubts.

---

8. Hagberg and Guelich, *The Critical Journey*, 82–83.
9. See McConkie, *Navigating the Mormon Faith Crisis*, 96.

Our ability to discern between commandment and cultural norm may cause us to become counter-culture. For example, a man may grow a long beard or wear a blue shirt to sacrament meeting, subtly declaring, "I will not be assimilated!"[10] We may also choose to abstain from some activities, even if our participation could benefit someone else. We may become argumentative and more apt to find fault in our leaders and others.

CRISIS AT THE YOUNG ADULT STAGE

Winters of faith at the Young Adult stage are cold and harsh. They can stem from burnout, hypocrisy, guilt, resistance to cultural assimilation, pride, or supplanting the will of God with our own. We realize that we can never do enough, know enough, or be enough to measure up to what we believe the Lord expects of us. The sacrifice is too great, the burden is too heavy, and we are too inadequate. The Lord's command to "be ye therefore perfect" (Matthew 4:48) hangs before us like an unmerciful magic mirror that accentuates all that is imperfect about us.

In these winters of faith, "the Lord God showeth us our weakness" (Jacob 4:7). He has promised, "If men come unto me I will show unto them their weakness. I give unto men weakness that they may be humble; and my grace is sufficient for all men that humble themselves before me; for if they humble themselves before me, and have faith in me, then will I make weak things become strong unto them" (Ether 12:27).

---

10. This quote is a reference to the television series *Star Trek: The Next Generation* (1987–1994) and the movie *Star Trek: First Contact* (1996). The Borg were cybernetic aliens who were perfectly unified in thought and action. As they sought to capture and integrate other species, they would declare, "We are the Borg. Lower your shields and surrender your ships. . . . Resistance is futile. You will be assimilated."

We may feel condemned like young Joseph Smith. He explained:

I was left to all kinds of temptations; and, mingling with all kinds of society, I frequently fell into many foolish errors, and displayed the weakness of youth, and the foibles of human nature; which, I am sorry to say, led me into divers temptations, offensive in the sight of God. In making this confession, no one need suppose me guilty of any great or malignant sins. A disposition to commit such was never in my nature. But I was guilty of levity, and sometimes associated with jovial company, etc., not consistent with that character which ought to be maintained by one who was called of God as I had been. But this will not seem very strange to any one who recollects my youth, and is acquainted with my native cheery temperament. In consequence of these things, I often felt condemned for my weakness and imperfections. (Joseph Smith—History 1:28–29)

If we can pray, we may petition the Lord like the Brother of Jared: "O Lord, and do not be angry with thy servant because of his weakness before thee; for we know that thou art holy and dwellest in the heavens, and that we are unworthy before thee; because of the fall our natures have become evil continually" (Ether 3:2).

The "Why Bothers"

It is during winters of faith at the Young Adult stage that we most often experience the "why bothers."

Why bother reading my scriptures? I'm not learning anything.

Why bother praying? He doesn't answer me.

Why bother magnifying my calling? I'm not good at it, and it only adds to my stress.

Why bother keeping the commandments? They're so confining, and I'll never be perfectly obedient.

Why bother attending church? I'm not sure I believe this anymore, and I don't feel the Spirit.

Why bother nourishing my seed of faith? All I feel is doubt, and my testimony is dying.

Enduring the Crisis

In these winters of faith, nourishment of the seed is imperative. The spiritual disciplines—for example, prayer, scripture study, and church attendance—strengthen our testimonies. Also, our level of desire for the disciplines signals the proximity of the Spirit. Nephi taught that "the Spirit . . . teacheth a man to pray. . . . The evil spirit teacheth not a man to pray, but teacheth him that he must not pray" (2 Nephi 32:8). If the Spirit encourages us to pray and Satan encourages us not to pray, we can measure how close we are to the Spirit by how much we desire to pray.

We could similarly consider our desire for the other disciplines, such as reading our scriptures, attending our church meetings, magnifying our callings, paying tithing, and attending the temple. Our desire for the disciplines increases as our distance from the Spirit decreases. The more we feel the Spirit, the more His influence becomes "delicious" (Alma 32:28) to us and the more we desire to do those things that will increase His influence in our lives. The disciplines both nourish our testimony and increase our desire for nourishment.

> *In the dark night, our doubt overcomes our desire, and we are left destitute of all that previously sustained us.*

The Approaching Dark Night

The true crisis of faith at the Young Adult stage is the dark night of the soul. In the dark night, our doubt overcomes our desire, and we are left destitute of all that previously sustained us. The "why bothers" may be the sunset in a winter of faith that signals the coming dark night. The dark night is the deconstruction of faith—faith in reverse. Faith is to hope, believe, and then act. As the dark night approaches, we may stop acting in faith, then stop believing, and then stop hoping. We may think, *Acting in faith isn't dispelling my doubts. So why bother? Why should I continue believing it will work? I no longer believe that it will, and I'm losing hope.* Therefore, the dark night of the soul is the deconstruction of faith that leaves us hopeless. Mormon taught, "Wherefore, if a man have faith he must needs have hope; for without faith there cannot be any hope" (Moroni 7:42). Hopelessness may cause us to seek hope somewhere else and lead us from all that we once held dear.

> *The dark night of the soul is the deconstruction of faith that leaves us hopeless.*

For some, the "why bothers" cause them to enter the dark night, while others enter the dark night and then begin to feel the "why bothers." Therefore, the "why bothers" may initiate the dark night or only be a symptom of it. Those who feel the "why bothers" as a symptom of the dark night may lose hope first and then stop believing and acting.

Key Point Summary

- The Young Adult stage is the most productive and rewarding stage of faith.
- The Young Adult stage feels like the pinnacle of spiritual development.
- Winters of faith in the Young Adult stage precede the dark night of the soul.

6

THE DARK NIGHT
OF THE SOUL

"When you come to the end of all the light you know, and it's time
to step into the darkness of the unknown, faith is knowing
that one of two things shall happen: either you will be given
something solid to stand on or you will be taught to fly."

—Edward Teller[1]

The dark night of the soul is not technically a stage of faith; it is the transition from the Young Adult stage to the Adult stage. However, because it is the preeminent transformational spiritual experience explored in this work, we will discuss it as if it were an independent stage of faith.

At some point in our lives, often between the ages of thirty and fifty, perhaps in the midst of a "mid-life crisis," we may transition gradually and then suddenly from the springtime of spiritual success into a cold, harsh winter of faith. We may believe we have been here

---

1. Edward Teller, "When you come to the end," AZ Quotes, accessed Nov. 9, 2022, https://www.azquotes.com/quote/351831.

before. After all, doubts were common through the earlier stages of our spiritual development. Buoyed by our faith, we sailed cautiously on our spiritual journey on the uncertain waters of life. We successfully navigated those jagged rocks of doubt that threatened to rip gashes in our testimony that has already weathered so many storms.

As night approaches, we may more earnestly delve into the disciplines (e.g., prayer, scripture study, and church attendance). For some, this nourishes the tender plant of faith. The burning in the bosom warms the spirit, and the soul is satisfied until the sun rises. In this case, it is indeed a cold, winter night—but not the dark night of the soul.

For others, the disciplines do little and the "why bothers" become more persistent. The night darkens and grows colder. The jagged rocks of doubt that previously jutted out sporadically in the distance loom larger in the fading light. As we cautiously press forward, they surround us, scraping the hardened hull of our faith. Doubts breach our testimony. We feel ourselves sinking into depths unknown. We are powerless to rescue ourselves.

In despair, we may cry out, "My God, my God, why hast thou forsaken me?" (Matthew 27:46). These words, uttered by the Savior as He hung impaled upon the cross, convey the confusion and sense of abandonment we feel in the dark night of the soul. David prophetically penned those words in the twenty-second Psalm and then added his own feelings of abandonment: "Why art thou so far from helping me, and from the words of my roaring? O my God, I cry in the daytime, but thou hearest not; and in the night season, and am not silent" (Psalm 22:1–2). "How long wilt thou forget me, O Lord? for ever? how long wilt thou hide thy face from me?" (Psalm 13:1). Joseph Smith cried out from Liberty Jail, "O God, where art thou? And where is the pavilion that covereth thy hiding place?" (Doctrine and Covenants 121:1).

In the dark night, we may feel God has abandoned us . . . or did we abandon Him? Or was He ever there? The two-sided coin of faith and doubt flips to the doubt side, and the doubts seem to overwhelm our faith. We question all that we believed and all that we have done. Has all been for naught? Have we failed? Have we been wrong all this time?

Many things can initiate the dark night. Hagberg and Guelich said:

> Suddenly, something in one's strict adherence is called into question. One of the foundation blocks crumbles. Perhaps someone considered to be a model of faith, a person of genuine piety, is exposed for being involved in an immoral or illegal activity. Perhaps another way of looking at the Scriptures or relating to God and life begins to catch one's attention. For example, specific doctrines about Scripture or the Church's infallibility come into question. Gnawing questions become more and more unmanageable, questions about what we believe and have believed and about how we live and why we do and do not do certain things. We are no longer able to ignore or repress them. They haunt us continually. So much so that we become aware of a larger gap in our lives of faith. We sense ourselves slipping more and more into a period of limbo.[2]

Jon Paulien explained that the dark night "could be precipitated by an external event, such as a rebellious child, the loss of a job or the death of a loved one. Sometimes it is precipitated by an internal event, such as physical illness or the resurfacing of an emotional trauma that was buried in the past up until this point. The dark night of the soul can simply be the sense that God has withdrawn His presence from our lives. We seek Him but we cannot find Him."[3] Paulien added:

---

2. Janet O. Hagberg and Robert A. Guelich, *The Critical Journey: Stages in the Life of Faith* (Salem, WI: Sheffield Publishing Company, 2005), 95.

3. Jon Paulien, "The Stages of Faith," The Battle of Armageddon, accessed Nov. 10, 2022, http://thebattleofarmageddon.com/stages_of_faith.html.

Most spiritual people feel distressed about this development. They believed that God's presence in the life should soothe the spirit, calm all fears, and bring joy to life's journey. The dark night seems like a wrong turn, a sign that they have somehow lost their spiritual way. They are tempted to "defeat it" or back away from it. The ego rises up to resist the experience. They may feel guilt or shame-ridden, feeling that they have deserved this experience. They may put themselves down or in some sense "enjoy" their misery.

[Some] may feel that dark nights are for the [other] people, not for them. They are supposed to be strong and confident in God. They feel the need to hide the darkness from others, even from themselves. They may feel all alone, as if no one else is going through an experience like it.[4]

But many faithful have experienced the dark night—some for moments, some for months. As noted, the Savior—the Son of God who had "communed with God" (Joseph Smith Translation, Matthew 4:2 [in Matthew 4:2, footnote c]) and was ministered to by an angel the night before (see Luke 22:43)—felt abandoned on the cross. Joseph Smith, who had seen both the Father and the Son, and who was visited by at least twenty-four different angels on countless occasions,[5] felt abandoned after he had been imprisoned almost four months in Liberty Jail.

Elijah "was an example of solid faith in the Lord" (Bible Dictionary, "Elijah"). He sealed the heavens so there would be no rain for three years (see 1 Kings 17:1), miraculously multiplied a meager amount of meal and oil so a widow of Zarephath and her son would not starve in the famine (see 1 Kings 17:8–16), raised the widow's son from the dead (see 1 Kings 17:17–23), and called down fire from heaven to consume a water-drenched offering to Jehovah (see 1 Kings 18:22–40).

---

4. Paulien, "The Stages of Faith."

5. See "24 Angels Who Visited Joseph Smith," LDS Living, Feb. 27, 2018, https://www.ldsliving.com/24-angels-who-visited-joseph-smith/s/79521.

Immediately thereafter, Jezebel threatened to kill him. He then fled into the wilderness and sat under a juniper tree. There he fell into deep depression and pled for the Lord to take his life (see 1 Kings 19:4), notwithstanding all the faith and miracles he had experienced up to that point.

Job, who "was perfect and upright, and one that feared God, and eschewed evil" (Job 1:1), learned that on a single day, his livestock, servants, and children were killed (see Job 1:16, 18–19). He was then afflicted with boils (Job 2:7), and his wife, who was certainly in the depths of her own dark night, spat at Job, "Dost thou still retain thine integrity? Curse God, and die!" (Job 2:9). His friends, who had come to comfort him, implied that his circumstances stemmed from his sinfulness (see Job 8:6; 15:5–6). One asked accusingly, "Is not thy wickedness great? And thine iniquities infinite?" (Job 22:5). Job, in the depths of depression in his dark night, wished he had never been born (see Job 3:11–13).

Peter, whose name means *rock*, implying solid and immovable, was described as "one of the greatest of men" (Bible Dictionary, "Peter"). He left all to follow Jesus (see Mark 1:16–18; 10:28), proclaimed that Jesus was "the Christ, the Son of the living God" (Matthew 16:16; John 6:69), walked on water (see Matthew 14:22–33), saw Jesus transfigured on the mount (see Matthew 17:2), was visited by Moses and Elijah (see Matthew 17:3), heard the voice of the Father (see Matthew 17:5), received the priesthood keys (see Matthew 16:19), and was the chief apostle and future leader of the Church. He swore he would die before denying Jesus (see Mark 14:31), but that same night, overwhelmed with doubt, confusion, and fear, he denied knowing the Savior three times (see Luke 22:54–61). Distraught by his doubt and denial, and in the depths of the dark night literally and spiritually, he "went out, and wept bitterly" (Luke 22:62).

Mother Teresa, who many consider a genuine example of Christ-like love and service, received revelations and saw visions from God that called her to a "call within a call."[6] She spent the remaining fifty years of her life in devoted service of the poorest of the poor as she simultaneously endured a severe dark night of the soul. In one letter she wrote, "In my soul I feel just that terrible pain of loss—of God not wanting me—of God not being God—of God not really existing."[7]

She described her dark night in this way: "This terrible sense of loss—this untold darkness—this loneliness—this continual longing for God—which gives me that pain deep down in my heart. Darkness is such that I really do not see—neither with my mind nor with my reason. The place of God in my soul is blank. There is not God in me. When the pain of longing is so great—I just long and long for God—and then it is that I feel—He does not want me."[8]

At another time, she wrote the following:

In the darkness . . . Lord, my God, who am I that you should forsake me? The child of your love—and now become as the most hated one. The one—you have thrown away as unwanted—unloved. I call, I cling, I want, and there is no one to answer. . . . Where I try to raise my thoughts to heaven, there is such convicting emptiness that those very thoughts return like sharp knives and hurt my very soul. Love—the word—it brings nothing. I am told God lives in me—and yet the reality of darkness and coldness and emptiness is so great that nothing touches my soul.[9]

6. "'I thirst!' Mother Teresa's Calling Within a Calling," Cinema Catechism, Sept. 29, 2010, https://cinemacatechism.blogspot.com/2010/09/i-thirst-mother-teresas-calling-within_22.html.

7. James Martin, "In My Soul: The long dark night of Mother Teresa," America: The Jesuit Review, Sept. 24, 2007, https://www.americamagazine.org/faith/2007/09/24/my-soul-long-dark-night-mother-teresa.

8. Martin, "In My Soul."

9. Mother Teresa and Brian Kolodiejchuk, Mother Teresa: Come Be My Light: The Private Writings of the Saint of Calcutta (Baltimore, MD: Image, 2009), 186–187.

These examples of the faithful in the dark night dispel the myth that those who doubt do so because of their desire for some sin. It is true that one can enter the dark night through disobedience, as was the case with King David. However, the evidence is overwhelming that the dark night of doubt also envelops the most worthy and faithful.

MY DARK NIGHT

The dark night of doubt also envelops the most worthy and faithful.

I am not one of the worthy or faithful, but I thought I would include my own story, hoping that it may resonate with some. I hesitate to share my personal experience, fearing that you will think more of me than I deserve or less of me than I would like. Also, for reasons you will later understand, I dislike drawing attention to myself and feel a twinge of discomfort each time I use the pronoun "I" in this book. Nevertheless, I will share my experience with the hope that some may relate my story to their own lives and benefit from the comparison. Here is the story of my trifecta of failure and my plunge into the depths of the dark night.

I was in the Young Adult stage of faith and climbing an imaginary leadership ladder in the Church. I was then serving as a bishop for the second time. There were many good members who sustained me and were anxiously engaged in the work of salvation. We accomplished much and were one of the stronger wards in our stake.

At home, my wife and I had a strong marriage. Our four children were healthy, dependable, and trustworthy. Two were in high school, one in middle school, and our youngest was in elementary school. Our goals for each of our three sons were that they would be ordained to each office of the Aaronic Priesthood, earn the Eagle Scout award in Boy Scouts, serve missions, and marry in the temple. Our goals for our daughter were that she would receive her Young Womanhood Recognition award, serve a mission if she desired, and marry in the temple.

At one point, my wife and I posted our family vision on the wall of our den. It was on the wall to the left of the television where we knew our children would see it every day. The vision included a picture of our family standing in front of the Dallas Texas Temple, the temple in which my wife and I were sealed. Our vision was that, regardless of where we lived at the time, we would one day return to the Dallas Temple after all of our children had been sealed to their spouses and take a similar family picture.

Four other pictures of our children taken at their baptisms surrounded that picture. Above the pictures were the words *Maranto Family Vision*. As each advanced toward the goal, we would replace their baptismal picture with a new picture that represented the most recent step they took toward our final vision of reuniting at the temple. For example, as one entered the mission field or married in the temple, we would replace the baptism picture with a picture from that event so we all could see that we were progressing to the goal. It felt like a clear and compelling vision that we hoped would daily remind our children of our desires for them.

A story I heard when I was a boy gave me the idea for the vision. A mother was saddened and perplexed that all three of her sons had left home to join the Navy instead of pursuing other opportunities for employment, continuing their education, serving missions, or even joining a different branch of service. Her bishop comforted her the best he could by explaining that young people feel the need to "break away" from what is expected of them, though he also thought their identical actions were unusual and hard to explain.

The bishop decided to visit the mother in her home. When he entered the living room, he noticed there was a single piece of art in the room—a large painting of a ship under full sail.

"There is your reason," he told the mother. "As your sons have grown up, you have told them every day through this painting of the romance and adventure of the sea. You have taught them well. No wonder they all joined the Navy."

The message of this true story is obvious. Our home environment—specifically, visual images in the home—has an impact on our lives.[10]

A few months after posting the vision on the wall, our oldest son, who had been ordained a priest and earned the Eagle Scout award, began to push away from the Church. He had read the Book of Mormon multiple times and had a deep knowledge of the gospel but had no testimony. He no longer wanted to attend church services.

I once heard an unconfirmed story attributed to Brigham Young. One of his sons did not want to attend church. The son declared, "I have agency. So I should be free to choose whether or not I go to church." Brigham Young answered, "You do have a choice. You can choose to go to church willingly or hog-tied in the back of my wagon."

We chose to take our son to church "hog-tied." We hoped something or someone at church would soften his heart and help him feel the Spirit. That never happened. Despite our fervent prayers and efforts, he only became more bitter. The contention on the pew was palpable. He sat in sacrament meeting with his arms crossed, regularly rolled his eyes at the speakers, and occasionally let out an audible "humph" in disagreement. We eventually let him stay home so we could once again enjoy the Spirit in sacrament meeting.

He was passionate about equality for the LGBTQ community. This was at the height of the Church's support of Proposition 8, a

---

10. Ed Maryon, "Look at Your Walls. What Do You See?", *Ensign*, Dec. 1973.

ballot proposition in California opposing same-sex marriage.[11] During that time, the Church also announced a policy declaring that those who entered same-sex marriages were apostates and subject to disciplinary action, and also that their children were not permitted to be blessed as infants or baptized until they were eighteen years old, and then only after receiving permission from the First Presidency.[12] We didn't want to discourage our son from supporting this marginalized community, but we were caught between supporting him and supporting the Church's firm stand against the LGTBQ initiatives. Our daughter, tenaciously vigilant in defense of equality, zealously stood with her brother and vehemently criticized the Church for opposing same-sex marriage, which fueled contention in our home.

Our dinner table, which had once been our sacred center of communion—the place where we prayed together and studied the scriptures as a family—became a battleground over faith and philosophy. The friendly, supportive conversations we once had were supplanted by heated contention. The Lord taught the Nephites, "For verily, verily I say unto you, he that hath the spirit of contention is not of me, but is of the devil, who is the father of contention, and he stirreth up the hearts of men to contend with anger, one with another" (3 Nephi 11:29). Our home became so filled with contention that we drove out the Spirit.

One day, I noticed that our family vision was not on the wall. I asked my wife about it, and she explained she could not bear to look at it anymore because it only reminded her that we were failing. Also,

---

11. See "Proposition 8," Howard University School of Law, accessed Nov. 8, 2022, https://library.law.howard.edu/civilrightshistory/lgbtq/prop8.

12. See Jennifer Dobner, "New Mormon policy makes apostates of married same-sex couples, bars children from rites," *The Salt Lake Tribune*, Nov. 6, 2015, https://archive.sltrib.com/article.php?id=3144035&itype=CMSID.

she didn't want it to be a lifelong reminder to our children that they had not met our expectations.

As time passed, our oldest son graduated high school, found a job, and moved into an apartment. I was released from serving as the bishop and called to serve as the stake Young Men president. As the stake president approached the end of his service, some said to me they believed I would be the next stake president—or at least in the presidency. That gratified my pride and vain ambition. Of course, "pride goeth before destruction, and an haughty spirit before a fall" (Proverbs 16:18).

My employment improved. I moved from a dead-end job to a job I loved that offered many opportunities. I was a training manager responsible for leadership development in my company. I helped about two thousand employees in leadership roles become better leaders. They would often approach me at company-wide meetings and express their appreciation for what they had learned from me. Some commented that what I had taught them was life-changing. It felt good to know I made a difference in their lives.

Though I was deeply disappointed that our oldest son had left the Church, I was feeling good about my life. My Social and Esteem needs were more than satisfied at church and work, and I was optimistic about our other three children.

Our daughter earned her Young Womanhood Recognition Award, graduated from high school and went to BYU–Idaho but was unhappy there. She applied for an internship at Disney World in Florida and was accepted. She moved to Florida and thereafter left the Church. Our third child was ordained a teacher but quit Boy Scouts just short of earning his Eagle Scout award. Like his older brother, he pushed against the Church. We required him to attend against his will, but since that approach was ineffective with our first son, we gave up after a comparatively short time, and he left the Church. Our youngest was ordained a deacon and only advanced to First Class in Boy Scouts. When he told us he no longer wanted to go to church, our will was depleted, our hope was lost, and we just surrendered and said, "Okay."

President Spencer W. Kimball once told the story of a father he met in the temple. President Kimball performed the sealing ordinance for the man's daughter. After the ceremony, the man approached President Kimball and the following conversation ensued:

> "Brother Kimball, my wife and I are common people and have never been successful, but we are immensely proud of our family." He continued, "This is the last of our eight children to come into this holy house for temple marriage. They, with their companions, are here to participate in the marriage of this, the youngest. This is our supremely happy day, with all of our eight children married properly. They are faithful to the Lord in church service, and the older ones are already rearing families in righteousness."
>
> I looked at his calloused hands, his rough exterior, and thought to myself, "Here is a real son of God fulfilling his destiny."
>
> "Success?" I said, as I grasped his hand. "That is the greatest success story I have heard. You might have accumulated millions in stocks and bonds, bank accounts, lands, industries, and still be quite a failure. You are fulfilling the purpose for which you were sent into this world by keeping your own lives righteous, bearing and rearing this great posterity, and training them in faith and works. Why, my dear folks, you are eminently successful. God bless you."[13]

If that was the "greatest success" in the Church, then my wife and I were the greatest failures. As David O. McKay taught, "No other success can compensate for failure in the home."[14] We would never reunite at the Dallas Temple. We could not even reunite in the chapel for sacrament meeting. When our first child fell away, we thought, *Even our perfect heavenly parents lost Lucifer.* When our second fell

---

13. Spencer W. Kimball, "Glimpses of Heaven," *Ensign*, Nov. 1971, 36–37.
14. Teachings of Presidents of the Church: David O. McKay (2003), 154.

away, we thought, *Even Lehi lost Laman and Lemuel.* When our third fell away, we thought, *A third part of our Father in Heaven's children followed Lucifer.* When our fourth fell away, we thought, *We are failures.*

My wife felt split between our children and the Church. The more closely she aligned with the tenets of the Church, the greater was the divide between her and our children. And she would never abandon her children. She transitioned from denial to anger in the stages of grief: denial, anger, bargaining, depression, and acceptance.[15] In the anger stage, she was angry at the Church for demanding so much of us. She was angry at me for spending so much time saving other people's children while ours were falling away. She was angry at herself for all she did or did not do, real or imagined, that caused our children to fall away.

She had graduated second in her high school class but postponed college and her career to be a stay-at-home mom so she could invest herself entirely in teaching and rearing our children. Therefore, most of her Social and Esteem needs were fulfilled in her family, and her Self-Actualization depended on what our family became. She was stripped of those most pressing needs as our children rejected what she taught them, criticized the values she professed, and left her feeling foolish for her beliefs.

The "why bothers" set in. She became discouraged and depressed (the fourth stage of grief). The dark night and all of the associated doubts enveloped her.

While my wife fell apart, I was well enough. Though I felt like a failure at home, my Social and Esteem needs were both fulfilled at work and church, and I was nearer to Self-Actualization than I had ever been. My pursuit of my career goals began to gain momentum.

---

15. See Kimberly Holland, "The Stages of Grief: What Do You Need to Know?," Healthline, last modified June 27, 2022, https://www.healthline.com/health/stages-of-grief.

My vision for myself was that I would one day author a best-selling leadership book and be a keynote speaker on a lecture circuit. Both were unlikely, but such is the nature of dreams. Through my employer, I had the opportunity to author a chapter in Ken Blanchard's book, *Servant Leadership in Action*. Ken Blanchard is a best-selling author/co-author of over sixty leadership books and is one of the most well-known and respected leadership experts. It was a privilege to collaborate with him on that book and to be named with him and other leadership gurus I had admired for years who also contributed to the book: John Maxwell, Brené Brown, Stephen M. R. Covey, Patrick Lencioni, Mark Miller, Simon Sinek, and others.

After writing that chapter, I began to write my first book on leadership. I was excited to take that crucial step toward achieving my personal vision. I worked on that book for over a year, pouring into it all the most important concepts I had learned about leadership through the previous twenty years. All the pieces were perfectly aligned. Blanchard would likely agree to write the foreword in my book. Blanchard's editor, Renee Broadwell, was advising me. Barrett-Koehler Publishers, who published *Servant Leadership in Action*, would likely be interested in this book because of my contribution to that book. I had all the right contacts and the timing was perfect!

At church, I was enjoying my calling as the stake Young Men president. As the stake president neared the end of his term, I tried not to aspire to that calling, though my need for Esteem and Self-Actualization caused me to anticipate the possibility.

Then my world fell apart. The trifecta of failure.

About the time my wife reached the peak of her anger and depression, I was interviewed as a candidate to be the next stake president. I remember thinking to myself, *I can't serve in the stake presidency. My wife is already angry and bitter because of the time and energy I've devoted to the Church. If I accept this calling, it will put undue strain on our marriage and we may not survive it.* Though I never mentioned my family circumstances in the interview, my demeanor and the Spirit conveyed I was not to serve in that presidency. Three other good men were called the following Sunday. After the meeting, I smiled and gracefully expressed my support of them as well-meaning friends said to me, "We thought for sure you would be in the presidency."

Soon thereafter, I was invited to participate in a stake committee formed to address "simplification." Our area authorities had encouraged us to simplify at church and in life to decrease stress and give more time back to families. I thought it ironic that we were forming a simplification committee. It seemed to me that forming a committee to discuss keeping things simple was a prime example of complicating the simple.

During the one and only committee meeting, I testified of the importance of balance between giving all our time, talents, and energy to the building up of the kingdom of God and giving to our families—though one could argue they are one in the same. During my years of service in the Church, I had earnestly striven to balance my Church service and work responsibilities with my family obligations, putting family first. I made it a priority to be at my children's birthday parties, concerts, sporting events, plays, and so on, though I missed more than I would like to admit due to work travel and, occasionally, Church responsibilities. I spent one-on-one time with each child. I even scheduled weekly one-on-one chats with each so we would have some time to talk about anything they wanted to talk about, though they didn't value that time so we discontinued them after only a few sessions. We had family prayer, family scripture study, and regular family home evenings. I thought I had earnestly put my family first, but my family disagreed.

In that committee meeting, I divulged that all our children had left the Church and that they, in part, blamed me for giving so much of myself to the Church. One of the members of the committee remarked sullenly, "That is the saddest story I have ever heard."

Soon thereafter, the stake president wisely released me from my stake calling so I could devote myself to my family. It was too little too late. That train had left the station, and there was little I could do then to help the Savior redeem my family. I was left without a calling and stripped of most of the Esteem I once felt at church.

At work, I was denied a promotion. Then, when I was ready to publish my book, my company declared it was their intellectual property and threatened to terminate my employment and sue me if I published it. I had received permission from my director before I wrote the book, but the company lawyers claimed he was not authorized to grant that permission on behalf of the company. I argued that I wrote the book on my own time: nights, weekends, and on vacation. But they claimed that, as a salaried employee, all my time was their time and anything I did relating to leadership belonged to them. I fought it and was fired.

I was a failure at home. I was a failure at church. I was a failure at work. The trifecta of failure.

I was unemployed for eleven months. We lived off of our savings, most of which were invested in stocks, which suffered a 15 percent decline in the quarter I lost my job, the worst decline in a decade.[16] While I was unemployed, we depleted one-third of what remained of our life savings after the stock market fell. The remaining funds were in my 401K, and I would have incurred about a 30 percent loss in taxes and penalties on any amount I withdrew from it.

---

16. See Fred Imbert, "US stocks post worst year in a decade as the S&P 500 falls more than 6% in 2018," CNBC, Dec. 21, 2018, https://www.cnbc.com/2018/12/31/stock-market-wall-street-stocks-eye-us-china-trade-talks.html.

The lawyers I hired for my intellectual property case against my former employer were more concerned about charging me by the minute for every phone call and email than about fighting for my cause. I spent over $10,000 on their services to secure my right to publish my book, but all they did after that investment and months of "working" on my case was counsel me to "publish it and see if they sue you." Of course, they were hoping the company *would* sue me because then I would have to pay them substantially more to argue the case.

I plummeted from being on the cusp of Self-Actualization, the highest level on Maslow's hierarchy, to the Physiological level, the lowest on that scale—from nearly achieving my personal vision to worrying over how I was going to put food on the table. My circumstances were minor compared to some who suffer greater loss, but it was sufficient to initiate my mid-life crisis and thrust me into a cold dark night of the soul.

After a few months without a calling, I was called to serve as the Primary pianist. I played mostly by ear and could read music but not well enough. I knew all the notes but couldn't sight-read. It was like knowing all the letters in the alphabet but not being able to read words.

The first Sunday I played was a humiliating experience. I tried playing just the melody with one hand, but I stumbled so badly I was surprised the children were able to sing a semblance of the songs. As luck would have it, I was called just a few months before the annual Primary program. I had to learn a half dozen or so new songs and play the piano in front an audience, which was terrifying for me. It was a tragic experience. Never has inspired music so effectively chased the Spirit out of a church than my piano-playing did that day. At one point, I was butchering a song so badly that I had to stop playing and let the children sing an entire verse a cappella until I regained my composure and was willing to bang out more discordant notes. This only added to my deepening discouragement.

I, like my wife, began to enter the dark night as our children fell away. The dark night darkened with each successive blow to my ego: being mocked by my children for the foolishness of my faith, my wife's gentle chiding for my devotion to the Church and the contention it caused in our home, not being called to serve in the stake presidency, the book I had spent a year pouring the best of my knowledge into being wrenched from my hands, being fired from my job and betrayed by people at work I thought were my friends, depletion of one-third of my life savings, the release from my calling and being left without a church responsibility for a time, and being humiliated at the piano in front of a congregation of people that only a year before considered me a respected leader.

In the cold, empty darkness, I cried out like David, "My God, my God, why hast thou forsaken me? why art thou so far from helping me?" (Psalm 22:1). Then . . . nothing. The Spirit that once whispered a somewhat steady stream of insight was silent. The heavens were closed. I was utterly alone. As many do in the dark night, I questioned, *Why did God abandon me . . . or did I abandon Him? Or was He ever there?*

In my dark night, I was beset by the "why bothers." I gradually stopped fasting, praying, and reading my scriptures. I distanced myself from the Spirit until I was almost "past feeling" (1 Nephi 17:45). Doubts crept in. Sin seemed less serious.

At church, I continued to go through the motions. On the outside, I was just as faithful as I had always been. Inside, I felt like an imposter, a hypocrite, a whited sepulcher (see Matthew 23:27–28).

I considered leaving the Church as others had done. I understood why they left. When the beliefs and practices no longer resonate with us, the sacrifices required for membership seem too burdensome, and the taxing pretense and perpetual pain preclude the spiritual benefits.

But since my youth, the Church had been the primary provider of my Social and Esteem needs, and so much of my identify was defined by my faith. As mentioned in the introduction of this book, leaving the Church would be to abandon all that I was and all that I held dear—my heritage, traditions, doctrines, hopes, friendships, and even family—to foray into a foreign and frightful future. So I chose to stay, hoping to "fake it till I make it." In retrospect, I see now that so much had been taken from me—my job, my book, my calling, and my savings—but the Church was one external thing I could choose to keep in my life.

I will share the rest of my story later in this book. For now, let's discuss the dark night in depth and how to endure it.

PROFOUND DOUBT

In the dark night, we experience profound doubt. We may doubt ourselves, the Church, its leaders, or God, and the firm faith we once stood upon disintegrates beneath our feet. This is perplexing for us because the Savior is supposed to be our firm foundation. Helaman taught his sons:

> And now, my sons, remember, remember that it is upon the rock of our Redeemer, who is Christ, the Son of God, that ye must build your foundation; that when the devil shall send forth his mighty winds, yea, his shafts in the whirlwind, yea, when all his hail and his mighty storm shall beat upon you, it shall have no power over you to drag you down to the gulf of misery and endless wo, because of the rock upon which ye are built, which is a sure foundation, a foundation whereon if men build they cannot fall. (Helaman 5:12)

Go Back, Go Out, or Go Forward

As the foundation dissolves beneath our feet, we seek firm footing again. The direction we move in may transform our faith or kill it. At this crossroads of faith, the options before us are to go back, go out, or go forward.

Most of us "go back." We regress to an earlier stage of faith, perhaps the Young Adult stage where we enjoyed success. We do the things we did to fortify our faith in that earlier stage. We go through the motions and outwardly appear faithful and fulfilled but inwardly are emptied of hope and filled with doubt. We know that something is different; something is wrong. The Primary answers (say your prayers, read your scriptures, attend church) have little effect, and we feel our faith dying from doubt. As our testimony withers, we mourn like the master of the vineyard in Zenos's allegory of the olive tree:

> But what could I have done more [for my faith]? Have I slackened mine hand, that I have not nourished it? Nay, I have nourished it, and I have digged about it, and I have pruned it, and I have dunged it; and I have stretched forth mine hand almost all the day long, and the end draweth nigh. And it grieveth me that I should [lose my testimony of the Church]. (Jacob 5:47)

As we go through the motions, we repeatedly find ourselves at the same crossroads, unsure if we should go back, go out, or go forward. Some of us keep going back to an earlier stage of faith in a perpetual cycle of spiritual stagnation, "ever learning, and never able to come to the knowledge of the truth" (2 Timothy 3:7).

Some of us "go out." We conclude that we have done all that we could to fortify our faith and that the Church has failed us. We asked and did not receive. We knocked and no doors opened. There was for us no manifestation, no vision, no dream, no angel, no thundering voice from heaven to shake us to our senses or still, small voice to soothe our soul. Only silence.

Our faith begins to feel like foolishness. The faults we find in the Church are magnified in our minds, and we become increasingly critical of it. We may browse through the plethora of the Church's online criticism, which becomes increasingly intriguing and compelling. Eventually, we conclude that our faith is not flawed—the Church is. Either God is not there, or God is nowhere because there *is* no God. Regardless, the Church is a fraud.

Fault-finding is the first sign of failing faith.

Fault-finding is easy since faults are plentiful in everyone—even in prophets and apostles. Moroni implored, "Condemn me not because of mine imperfection, neither my father, because of his imperfection, neither them who have written before him; but rather give thanks unto God that he hath made manifest unto you our imperfections, that ye may learn to be more wise than we have been" (Mormon 9:31). It can be instructive for us to recognize their faults, but it is destructive for us to discredit perfect doctrine because of imperfect people.

Fault-finding is the first sign of failing faith. Joseph Smith explained, "I will give you one of the Keys of the mysteries of the Kingdom. It is an eternal principle, that has existed with God from all eternity: That man who rises up to condemn others, finding fault with the Church, saying that they are out of the way, while he himself is righteous, then know assuredly, that that man is in the high road to apostasy; and if he does not repent, will apostatize, as God lives."[17]

President George Q. Cannon further clarified that there may be times when members of the Church disagree with the leaders. He explained that disagreement is not necessarily apostasy unless they

_____

17. *Teachings of Presidents of the Church: Joseph Smith* (2007), 318.

publish their disagreements with the intent to divide people and create discord. He said:

> We could conceive of a man honestly differing in opinion from the Authorities of the Church and yet not be an apostate; but we could not conceive of a man publishing these differences of opinion and seeking by arguments, sophistry and special pleading to enforce them upon the people to produce division and strife and to place the acts and counsels of the Authorities of the Church, if possible, in a wrong light, and not be an apostate, for such conduct was apostasy as we understood the term. We further said that while a man might honestly differ in opinion from the Authorities through a want of understanding, he had to be exceedingly careful how he acted in relation to such differences, or the adversary would take advantage of him, and he would soon become imbued with the spirit of apostasy and be found fighting against God and the authority which He had placed here to govern His Church.[18]

We believe that the prophets speak the mind and will of God. The Lord stated, "Whether by mine own voice or by the voice of my servants, it is the same" (Doctrine and Covenants 1:38). However, some have concluded that everything a prophet says or does represents the revealed mind and will of God. This is not true. Elder Dallin H. Oaks explained.

> Revelations from God—the teachings and directions of the Spirit—are not constant. We believe in continuing revelation, not continuous revelation. We are often left to work out problems without the dictation or specific direction of the Spirit. That is part of the experience we must have in mortality. Fortunately, we are never out of our Savior's sight, and if our judgment leads us to actions beyond the limits of what is permissible and if we are

---

18. George Q. Cannon, *Gospel Truth* (Salt Lake City: Deseret Book, 1974), 493.

listening to the still, small voice, the Lord will restrain us by the promptings of his Spirit.[19]

The belief that everything prophets say or do is the revealed will of God paints some members of the Church into a corner and leaves them without recourse when the prophets err. And they *do* err. President Dieter F. Uchtdorf explained:

> There have been times when members or leaders in the Church have simply made mistakes. There may have been things said or done that were not in harmony with our values, principles, or doctrine. I suppose the Church would be perfect only if it were run by perfect beings. God is perfect, and His doctrine is pure. But He works through us—His imperfect children—and imperfect people make mistakes.[20]

In 1905, B. H. Roberts, a Church historian and General Authority, explained:

> I think it a reasonable conclusion to say that constant, never-varying inspiration is not a factor in the administration of the affairs of the Church; not even good men, no, not even though they be prophets or other high officials of the Church, are at all times and in all things inspired of God. It is only occasionally, and at need, that God comes to their aid.
>
> That there have been unwise things done in the Church by good men, men susceptible at times to the inspiration of the Spirit of God, we may not question. Many instances in the history of the Church, through three quarters of a century, prove it, and it would be a solecism to say that God was the author of those unwise, not to say positively foolish, things that have been done. For these things men must stand responsible, not God.
>
> It is well nigh as dangerous to claim too much for the inspiration of God, in the affairs of men, as it is to claim too little. By the first,

---

19. Dallin H. Oaks, "Teaching and Learning by the Spirit," *Ensign*, March 1997.

20. Dieter F. Uchtdorf, "Come, Join with Us," *Ensign* or *Liahona*, Nov. 2013, 22.

men are led into superstition, and into blasphemously accrediting their own imperfect actions, their blunders, and possibly even their sins, to God; and by the second, they are apt to altogether eliminate the influence of God from human affairs; I pause in doubt as to which conclusion would be the worse.[21]

Despite their faults, errors, blunders, and sins, we are assured that God will not permit the apostles and prophets to lead the Church astray (see Official Declaration 1). It is incumbent upon us to prayerfully discern when they speak and act under the direction of God and when they do not. When they falter, we remember they are also on their own perilous spiritual journey and they need our kindness, love, forgiveness, and support just like everyone else.

As we find faults, we may begin to share what we find. We may share with our spouse, relatives, or friends, or with strangers online. We become more emboldened as others ratify our concerns. Our fault-finding turns into criticizing and evil speaking of the Lord's anointed. Eventually, leaving the Church evolves from a consideration to a moral obligation. It would be hypocritical to continue in the Church when we believe it is a false church with false prophets and practices.

However, the thought of leaving pains us. For many of us, the Church defines much of our identity. Our values, hopes, dreams, life purpose, ambitions, friendships, and family members are tied to the Church. Leaving it is leaving who we love, who we are, what we do, and where we wanted to go. It could threaten some of our most valued relationships. Some of our closest friends will shake their heads in disappointment, leaders will discuss our downfall in ward council, and we will be on "the list" as somebody's project. Well-meaning leaders and members will minister to us, hoping to save the lost sheep.

---

21. B. H. Roberts, "Relation of Inspiration and Revelation to Church Government," *Improvement Era*, Mar. 1905, 367.

And what if we are wrong? What if we later discover we were deceived and desire to return to the Church, humbled and embarrassed by our weak-mindedness? Would it not be better to stay in the Church for now, just in case?

Unsure what to do next, some of us repeat the process of regression and "go back" to an earlier stage of faith. Others "go out." We explore alternatives for spirituality. We may consider other Christian denominations, non-Christian worldviews (e.g., Buddhism, Hinduism), or new age spirituality (e.g., meditation, astrology, paganism) to fill the spiritual void that remains as we extricate the Church from our lives. We may convince ourselves that a church is unnecessary to maintain our relationship with God. Even the Savior said, "For where two or three are gathered together in my name, there am I in the midst of them" (Matthew 18:20). Can we not gather in His name in our homes with our families and friends or with like-minded people online and enjoy His presence?

We then leave the Church convinced we can "work out [our] own salvation" (Mormon 9:27). For a time, we may enjoy liberation from the confining commandments and experience a spike of spirituality. But like a log removed from the fire, the flame we carry dwindles and eventually burns out without the fuel found only in the Church.

We may decide there is no God and subscribe to the teachings of Korihor, who declared that faith in Christ is "a foolish and a vain hope" (Alma 30:13), that the doctrines of Christ are "foolish traditions" (verse 14), and that belief in Him is "the effect of a frenzied" and deranged mind (verse 16). At best, we become what Elder Neal A. Maxwell called "sophisticated neutrals."[22] We view the Church as a forum for the foolish and uneducated and smile condescendingly, feigning support of those who find joy in it. At worst, we fight against

---

22. Neal A. Maxwell, *Deposition of a Disciple* (Salt Lake City: Deseret Book, 1976), 88.

the Church and become an enemy to God, a child of perdition, and commit the only unforgiveable sin of blasphemy against the Holy Ghost. As Joseph Smith explained:

> All sins shall be forgiven, except the sin against the Holy Ghost; for Jesus will save all except the sons of perdition. What must a man do to commit the unpardonable sin? He must receive the Holy Ghost, have the heavens opened unto him, and know God, and then sin against Him. After a man has sinned against the Holy Ghost, there is no repentance for him. . . . And from that time he begins to be an enemy . . . to this work. . . . He gets the spirit of the devil— the same spirit that they had who crucified the Lord of Life—the same spirit that sins against the Holy Ghost. You cannot save such persons; you cannot bring them to repentance; they make open war, like the devil, and awful is the consequence.[23]

Some have supposed few people commit this unforgivable sin. But Joseph Fielding Smith explained, "Evidently many among us have made a dreadful mistake . . . in thinking that the sons of perdition will be few. We have heard it said at times that they will be so few that they probably could be 'counted on the fingers of one hand.' Where this thought originated we may not know. From the reading of the scriptures it appears that there will be a large number."[24]

Some who have "gone out" engage in open war against the Lord, His prophets, and the Church. If they do so contrary to a previously received, undeniable manifestation of the Holy Ghost, there will be no forgiveness for them. As the Guide to the Scriptures states, "Sons of perdition include . . . those who [in mortality] served Satan and

---

23. Joseph Fielding Smith and Richard C. Galbraith, *Scriptural Teachings of the Prophet Joseph Smith* (Salt Lake City: Deseret Book, 1993), 401–402.

24. Joseph Fielding Smith, *Answers to Gospel Questions* (Salt Lake City: Deseret Book, 1957), 78.

turned utterly against God."[25] Fortunately, most of those who "go out" do not descend to that depth of depravity.

At the crossroads of faith, most "go back," some "go out," and few "go forward." The reason few "go forward" is because the way forward is dark and foreboding and the path is obscured. It lies directly in front of us but is fogged over by the prevailing myths about faith and doubt. The myth that doubt is the absence of faith and that faith means to not doubt. The myth that doubt is taboo among faithful believers. The myth that people always cause their own doubts. The myth that one who doubts is steeped in sin. All these myths, and others, obscure the path ahead and lead most to believe that their only options are to "go back" or "go out."

However, the Lord wants us to "go forward." The path forward leads to significant spiritual transformation. Stepping forward allows our Father to envelop us in His divinely designed chrysalis that transforms us into all He needs us to be. We must step into the fog and allow the dark night to close upon us.

Paulien explained that "this darkness is actually a call from God; it is a positive sign. It is a sign that God is deeply engaged in your life. While doubt can be a negative thing for spiritual life, the dark night of the soul is a doubt that can lead to deeper faith."[26] Hagberg and Guelich stated:

> This experience is perhaps the most poignant example of mystery in the whole journey of faith. There is a deep sense of God at work in us in the [dark night], and, at the same time, we are at a loss to describe it. We enter [the dark night] with fear and trepidation, but we become less afraid of being afraid because of God's leading. We are on holy ground. We are experiencing a pivotal moment when

25. Guide to the Scriptures, "Sons of Perdition," scriptures. ChurchofJesusChrist.org.

26. Jon Paulien, "The Stages of Faith," The Battle of Armageddon, accessed Nov. 10, 2022, http://thebattleofarmageddon.com/stages_of_faith.html.

we feel drawn to surrender; knowing it will not be easy, but it will be worthwhile. We are dying to self and waiting to be reborn."[27]

The darkness of the dark night is intense doubt. We doubt the Church. We doubt God. We doubt others. We doubt ourselves. We doubt who we were. We doubt who we are. We doubt who we were meant to be. Our doubts paralyze us, and the myths about doubt cause us to feel shame and guilt.

> *Every dark night is similar and every dark night is different.*

The dark night of the soul feels contrary to all we were taught about spiritual light and darkness. The Lord explained:

And that which doth not edify is not of God, and is darkness.

That which is of God is light; and he that receiveth light, and continueth in God, receiveth more light; and that light groweth brighter and brighter until the perfect day.

And again, verily I say unto you, and I say it that you may know the truth, that you may chase darkness from among you. (Doctrine and Covenants 50:23–25)

Jesus taught, "I am come a light into the world, that whosoever believeth on me should not abide in darkness" (John 12:46). He promised, "I am the light of the world: he that followeth me shall not walk in darkness, but shall have the light of life" (John 8:12).

Why are we in darkness when we have followed the Light? God has betrayed us . . . if there even is a God.

We are lost. We are confused. We are hurt. We lose hope and our faith is dying. As noted earlier, the dark night of the soul is the deconstruction of faith that leaves us hopeless. "For without faith there cannot be any hope" (Moroni 7:42).

---

27. Janet O. Hagberg and Robert A. Guelich, *The Critical Journey: Stages in the Life of Faith* (Salem, WI: Sheffield Publishing Company, 2005), 114–115.

Enduring the Dark Night

The Father tailors the dark night for each individual. Therefore, every dark night is similar and every dark night is different. To fully benefit from the dark night, each person must "work out their own salvation" (Mormon 9:27) and find their own path through it.

Enduring the dark night is not merely groping in the darkness and hoping for dawn. It is doing all we can to supplicate the Spirit to periodically and momentarily part the darkness just enough so we can see the Light in the distance and get our bearings.

It should be noted that darkness is the default. Before the Creation, "the earth was without form, and void" (Genesis 1:2), and darkness filled the expanse of space. "Darkness reigned" (Abraham 4:2) before "God said, Let there be light: and there was light" (Genesis 1:3). Light always dispels darkness, but there must be a source. Where there is no source of light, darkness reigns because darkness is the default. Therefore, in the dark night, we must continually seek the source of light. Jesus said, "I am the true light that lighteth every man that cometh into the world" (Doctrine and Covenants 93:2). In the dark night, we must seek earnestly for the Light of Christ or else darkness will prevail and we will lose our way, wander off, and be lost (see 1 Nephi 8:23).

Some of the most common ways to supplicate the Spirit and seek the Light in the dark night are provided here. One may find all, most, or a few of these helpful. Most will discover additional solutions that are a boon to them.

Light always dispels darkness, but there must be a source. Where there is no source of light, darkness reigns because darkness is the default.

To endure the dark night, we can:

1. Redefine the crisis
2. Surrender to the will of God

3. Shed selfishness
4. Seek a mentor
5. Commune with the Spirit
6. Be humble
7. Accept ourselves

Redefine the Crisis

The first step to enduring the dark night of the soul is to see the dark night not as a *crisis* of faith but as a *transition* to greater faith. Thomas McConkie explained, "*Crisis* implies a state of emergency. *Transition*, however, points to a deeper calm—even a sense of discovery as one chapter ends and another begins. As is often the case, a

> **See the dark night not as a crisis of faith but as a transition to greater faith.**

subtle language cue can point us to a developmental shift. In this case, one is no longer crying for a life preserver but swimming calmly with the current."[28]

The dark night is, for some, an essential phase in the stages of spiritual development. Seeing the dark night as a transition to the next stage of faith is to acknowledge that God has not abandoned us and is intimately involved in our lives, transforming us into the best version of ourselves. It is to recognize that the dark night of the soul is not the death of our faith but the birth of stronger faith, for "to grow as humans, we must first die to a smaller self."[29] Just as the acorn is cracked and broken before it becomes a majestic oak tree, so too are we nearly broken in the dark night to become all our Father intends for us to be.

---

28. Thomas Wirthlin McConkie, *Navigating the Mormon Faith Crisis: A Simple Development Map* (Salt Lake City: Mormon Stages, 2015), 118.

29. McConkie, *Navigating the Mormon Faith Crisis*, 5.

Our Father in Heaven perfectly tailors the dark night of the soul to fit us individually. We must "press forward" (2 Nephi 31:20), trusting that He "will not suffer [us] to be [tried] above that [we] are able; but will with the [trial] also make a way to escape, that [we] may be able to bear it" (1 Corinthians 10:13).

To be clear, God does not try us above what we can endure *spiritually*. The dark night of the soul is a *spiritual* trial. In other words, He will not try us to the point that we are incapable of retaining our faith. However, some endure horrific experiences (e.g., sexual or physical abuse) that break them physically, emotionally, and mentally. Our Father in Heaven does not expect them to "be able to bear it" (1 Corinthians 10:13). Instead, He expects those around them to love them, lift them, and help them bear it.

The dark night of the soul will span a mere moment of time but will be a blessing for eternity. Consider, for example, the words of the Savior to Joseph Smith in his dark night in Liberty Jail:

> My son, peace be unto thy soul; thine adversity and thine afflictions shall be but a small moment. (Doctrine and Covenants 121:7)
>
> If thou art called to pass through tribulation . . . if the heavens gather blackness, and all the elements combine to hedge up the way; and above all, if the very jaws of hell shall gape open the mouth wide after thee, know thou, my son, that all these things shall give thee experience, and shall be for thy good.
>
> The Son of Man hath descended below them all. Art thou greater than he? (Doctrine and Covenants 122:5, 7–8)

The dark night of the soul will span a mere moment of time but will be a blessing for eternity.

Elder Jeffrey R. Holland gave a talk titled "Waiting on the Lord" in the October 2020 general conference. In that talk, he said:

> The point? The point is that faith means trusting God in good times and bad, even if that includes some suffering until we see His arm

revealed in our behalf. That can be difficult in our modern world when many have come to believe that the highest good in life is to avoid all suffering, that no one should ever anguish over anything. But that belief will never lead us to "the measure of the stature of the fulness of Christ."

With apologies to Elder Neal A. Maxwell for daring to modify and enlarge something he once said, I too suggest that "one's life . . . cannot be both faith-filled and stress-free." It simply will not work "to glide naively through life," saying as we sip another glass of lemonade, "Lord, give me all thy choicest virtues, but be certain not to give me grief, nor sorrow, nor pain, nor opposition. Please do not let anyone dislike me or betray me, and above all, do not ever let me feel forsaken by Thee or those I love. In fact, Lord, be careful to keep me from all the experiences that made Thee divine. And then, when the rough sledding by everyone else is over, please let me come and dwell with Thee, where I can boast about how similar our strengths and our characters are as I float along on my cloud of comfortable Christianity."

My beloved brothers and sisters, Christianity is comforting, but it is often not comfortable. The path to holiness and happiness here and hereafter is a long and sometimes rocky one. It takes time and tenacity to walk it. But, of course, the reward for doing so is monumental.[30]

When we redefine the crisis as a transition to greater faith, we recognize that the dark night is for our good and will help transform us into what the Lord intends for us to be.

Surrender to the Will of God

In the dark night, we must let go and let God. "Let go and let God" is a popular Christian mantra. The equivalent in the scriptures is to "be still, and know that I am God" (Psalm 46:10). The message is for us to simply trust in Him and permit Him to do what He will

---

30. Jeffrey R. Holland, "Waiting on the Lord," *Ensign* or *Liahona*, Nov. 2020, 116.

in our lives. It is to surrender to the will of God, supplanting "my will be done" with "Thy will be done" (Luke 22:42).

From childhood, we are taught to pursue our dreams and never give up. We envision who and what we want to become and set our course to that end. We then spend our lives purposefully pursuing that goal, convinced we can do anything we set our minds to. Some become all they hoped they would be and then enter the dark night of the soul. Others' dreams are dashed and they are thrust into the dark night.

If that happens to us, we are left bewildered. Didn't God promise that if we paid our tithes and offerings, He would open to us the windows of heaven and pour out so many blessings there would not be room to receive them (see Malachi 3:19)? Did He not say that if we build His kingdom, He would fulfill our needs and provide for our wants (see Matthew 6:38)? Did He not assure us that if we ask, we would receive, and if we knock, doors would be opened for us (see Matthew 7:7)? Where is He now? Why has He let this happen to us?

Elder Hugh B. Brown, who was in the Quorum of the Twelve Apostles, shared this story. It is a perfect example of one suffering from dashed dreams and then surrendering to the will of God.

> I was living up in Canada. I had purchased a farm. It was run-down.
>
> I went out one morning and saw a currant bush. It had grown up over six feet high. It was going all to wood. There were no blossoms and no currants. I was raised on a fruit farm in Salt Lake before we went to Canada, and I knew what ought to happen to that currant bush. So I got some pruning shears and went after it, and I cut it down, and pruned it, and clipped it back until there was nothing left but a little clump of stumps.
>
> It was just coming daylight, and I thought I saw on top of each of these little stumps what appeared to be a tear, and I thought the currant bush was crying. I was kind of simpleminded (and I haven't entirely gotten over it), and I looked at it, and smiled, and said, "What are you crying about?" You know, I thought I heard

that currant bush talk. And I thought I heard it say this: "How could you do this to me? I was making such wonderful growth. I was almost as big as the shade tree and the fruit tree that are inside the fence, and now you have cut me down. Every plant in the garden will look down on me, because I didn't make what I should have made. How could you do this to me? I thought you were the gardener here."

That's what I thought I heard the currant bush say, and I thought it so much that I answered. I said, "Look, little currant bush, I *am* the gardener here, and I know what I want you to be. I didn't intend you to be a fruit tree or a shade tree. I want you to be a currant bush, and some day, little currant bush, when you are laden with fruit, you are going to say, 'Thank you, Mr. Gardener, for loving me enough to cut me down, for caring enough about me to hurt me. Thank you, Mr. Gardener.'"

Time passed. Years passed, and I found myself in England. I was in command of a cavalry unit in the Canadian Army. I had made rather rapid progress as far as promotions are concerned, and I held the rank of field officer in the British Canadian Army. And I was proud of my position. And there was an opportunity for me to become a general. I had taken all the examinations. I had the seniority. There was just one man between me and that which for ten years I had hoped to get, the office of general in the British Army. I swelled up with pride. And this one man became a casualty, and I received a telegram from London. It said: "Be in my office tomorrow morning at 10:00," signed by General Turner in charge of all Canadian forces.

I called in my valet, my personal servant. I told him to polish my buttons, to brush my hat and my boots, and to make me look like a general because that is what I was going to be. He did the best he could with what he had to work on, and I went up to London.

I walked smartly into the office of the General, and I saluted him smartly, and he gave me the same kind of a salute a senior officer usually gives—a sort of "Get out of the way, worm!" He said, "Sit down, Brown." Then he said, "I'm sorry I cannot make the appointment. You are entitled to it. You have passed all the examinations. You have the seniority. You've been a good officer, but I can't make the appointment. You are to return to Canada and become a training officer and a transport officer. Someone else will be made a general." That for which I had been hoping and praying for ten years suddenly slipped out of my fingers.

Then he went into the other room to answer the telephone, and I took a soldier's privilege of looking on his desk. I saw my personal history sheet. Right across the bottom of it in bold, block-type letters was written, "THIS MAN IS A MORMON." We were not very well liked in those days. When I saw that, I knew why I had not been appointed. I already held the highest rank of any Mormon in the British Army.

He came back and said, "That's all, Brown." I saluted him again, but not quite as smartly. I saluted out of duty and went out.

I got on the train and started back to my town, 120 miles away, with a broken heart, with bitterness in my soul. And every click of the wheels on the rails seemed to say, "You are a failure. You will be called a coward when you get home. You raised all those Mormon boys to join the army, then you sneak off home." I knew what I was going to get, and when I got to my tent, I was so bitter that I threw my cap and my saddle brown belt on the cot. I clinched my fists and I shook them at heaven. I said, "How could you do this to me, God? I have done everything I could do to measure up. There is nothing that I could have done—that I should have done—that I haven't done. How could you do this to me?" I was as bitter as gall.

And then I heard a voice, and I recognized the tone of this voice. It was my own voice, and the voice said, "I am the gardener here. I know what I want you to do." The bitterness went out of my soul, and I fell on my knees by the cot to ask forgiveness for my ungratefulness and my bitterness. While kneeling there I heard a song being sung in an adjoining tent. A number of Mormon boys met regularly every Tuesday night. I usually met with them. We would sit on the floor and have a Mutual Improvement Association. As I was kneeling there, praying for forgiveness, I heard their voices singing:

It may not be on the mountain height
Or over the stormy sea;

It may not be at the battle's front
My Lord will have need of me;
But if, by a still, small voice he calls
To paths that I do not know,
I'll answer, dear Lord, with my hand in thine:
I'll go where you want me to go. (*Hymns*, no. 270)

I arose from my knees a humble man. And now, almost fifty years later, I look up to him and say, "Thank you, Mr. Gardener, for cutting me down, for loving me enough to hurt me." I see now that it was wise that I should not become a general at that time, because if I had I would have been senior officer of all western Canada, with a lifelong, handsome salary, a place to live, and a pension when I'm no good any longer, but I would have raised my six daughters and two sons in army barracks. They would no doubt have married out of the Church, and I think I would not have amounted to anything. I haven't amounted to very much as it is, but I have done better than I would have done if the Lord had let me go the way I wanted to go.

I wanted to tell you that oft-repeated story because there are many of you who are going to have some very difficult experiences: disappointment, heartbreak, bereavement, defeat. You are going to be tested and tried to prove what you are made of. I just want you to know that if you don't get what you think you ought to get, remember, "God is the gardener here. He knows what he wants you to be." Submit yourselves to his will. Be worthy of his blessings, and you will get his blessings.[31]

To survive the dark night, we must surrender to the will of God and remember that He is the gardener here. He is helping us to become all He wants us to be and, in the end, all we want to be. We may not yet know what that is, but we must trust that He does and that the path He chooses for us will be for our good and benefit. We must trust in the Good Shepherd.

The Lord is my shepherd; I shall not want.

---

31. Hugh B. Brown, "The Currant Bush," *New Era*, Jan. 1973.

He maketh me to lie down in green pastures: he leadeth me beside the still waters.

He restoreth my soul: he leadeth me in the paths of righteousness for his name's sake.

Yea, though I walk through the valley of the shadow of death, I will fear no evil: for thou art with me; thy rod and thy staff they comfort me.

Thou preparest a table before me in the presence of mine enemies: thou anointest my head with oil; my cup runneth over.

Surely goodness and mercy shall follow me all the days of my life: and I will dwell in the house of the Lord forever. (Psalm 23:1–6)

Shed Selfishness

To endure the dark night, we must shed our selfishness. Selfishness is instilled in us by nature and nurture. It is embedded in our biology as an instinct for self-preservation—the survival instinct. Also, we are taught to be selfish from the moment we take our first breath. We cry a little and someone comes running to feed us, change our diaper, cuddle us, entertain us, or grant our other needs or wants. Our instinct for self-preservation evolves into self-adulation, for it seems everyone and everything exists to serve us.

But then the fateful day arrives. We are sitting on the floor playing with another child. That child takes our toy. Of course, we will not allow that, so we attempt to wrench it from the child's hands. He does not relinquish the toy, so we let out a cry calling on our servants to discipline the audacious thief and return the toy to us. Our mother comes running just as she should, but then something happens that shakes the very foundation of our perfect existence. She puts her hands on her hips then wags a finger at us and says, "Now, you need to share."

Excuse me? we think to ourselves. *Perhaps you have forgotten how this works. I cry and you come and provide whatever I want. This relationship has worked perfectly for my entire life. There is no need to change the rules now.*

But the rules *have* changed, and suddenly we are expected to be selfless. We then spend the rest of our lives countering our instinct and deprogramming our selfishness in order to be a contributing member of society.

Shedding our selfishness is one of the most important steps in our spiritual transformation. In the dark night, our facade is stripped from us and we see ourselves as we really are. We are called to confess that much of our serving in the Church has been self-serving. We admit that our desperate, self-serving quest to satisfy our Social, Esteem, and Self-Actualization needs have been the motive for much of our "selfless" service. Perhaps we served quietly in the background because we liked the good feeling we get when we help others. Perhaps we, like the Pharisees, served "to be seen of men" (Matthew 23:5), to be valued, honored, and accepted. All self-serving.

Immediately after the Lord commanded, "Be ye therefore perfect, even as your Father which is in heaven is perfect" (Matthew 5:48), He taught that shedding our self-serving nature is the first step on our path to perfection:

Take heed that ye do not your alms before men, to be seen of them: otherwise ye have no reward of your Father which is in heaven.

Therefore when thou doest thine alms, do not sound a trumpet before thee, as the hypocrites do in the synagogues and in the streets, that they may have glory of men. Verily I say unto you, They have their reward.

But when thou doest alms, let not thy left hand know what thy right hand doeth:

That thine alms may be in secret: and thy Father which seeth in secret himself shall reward thee openly.

And when thou prayest, thou shalt not be as the hypocrites are: for they love to pray standing in the synagogues and in the corners of the streets, that they may be seen of men. Verily I say unto you, They have their reward.

But thou, when thou prayest, enter into thy closet, and when thou hast shut thy door, pray to thy Father which is in secret; and thy Father which seeth in secret shall reward thee openly.

Moreover when ye fast, be not, as the hypocrites, of a sad countenance: for they disfigure their faces, that they may appear unto men to fast. Verily I say unto you, They have their reward.

But thou, when thou fastest, anoint thine head, and wash thy face;

That thou appear not unto men to fast, but unto thy Father which is in secret: and thy Father, which seeth in secret, shall reward thee openly.

No man can serve two masters: for either he will hate the one, and love the other; or else he will hold to the one, and despise the other. Ye cannot serve God and mammon. (Matthew 6:1–6, 16–18, 24)

In the dark night, we have to recognize when we have been self-serving, not serving. We have to confess that even in our Church service, we have been serving two masters: God and ourselves. This is most evident as we consider our activity in the Young Adult stage of faith.

Is it possible to shed all selfishness? Probably not. Selfishness is so deeply embedded in our biology and programming that most of us cannot entirely root it out. Nor should we try. After all, our self-serving motives have spurred us to "be anxiously engaged in a good cause, and do many things of [our] own free will, and bring to pass much righteousness" (Doctrine and Covenants 58:27). However, as a result of our spiritual transformation in the dark night, we become acutely aware of our self-serving motives. "Thy will be done" (Moses 4:2) then takes on a deeper meaning. We transcend beyond "I will do what you want me to do" to "I will do what you want me to do with an eye single to Thy glory, and the glory be Thine forever" (see Doctrine and Covenants 4:5; Moses 4:2). When we feel ourselves supplanting our glory with His, we recognize our selfishness and repent of it as with any other sin. As we do so, we more earnestly serve one Master and become more "perfect in Christ" (Moroni 10:32). Then our Father rewards us openly during this life or in the life to come (see Matthew 6:4).

SEEK A MENTOR

When in the dark night, we should seek a mentor who has experienced the dark night—those who are in the Adult or Senior stages of faith. We can recognize them because they are not caught up in the culture of the Church. They are anxiously engaged in the work of salvation but disinterested in programs. Instead, they serve quietly, working one on one with people just as the Savior did. They are "submissive, meek, humble, patient, [and] full of love" (Mosiah 3:19).

Some have endured the dark night independently. They suffered in silence and "press[ed] forward with a steadfastness in Christ" (2 Nephi 31:20) until morning came. Too many have not successfully endured the dark night. Lehi spoke of this as he shared his vision of the tree of life: "And it came to pass that there arose a mist of darkness; yea, even an exceedingly great mist of darkness, insomuch that they who had commenced in the path did lose their way, that they wandered off and were lost" (1 Nephi 8:23). As Nephi explained, "The mists of darkness are the temptations of the devil, which blindeth the eyes, and hardeneth the hearts of the children of men, and leadeth them away into broad roads, that they perish and are lost" (1 Nephi 12:17).

In the scriptures, temptation can mean allurement to sin, but in most cases, temptation in the scriptures means to be tried, proven, or tested.[32] Therefore, the mists of darkness are, in part, the trials and tests that naturally occur in life (see Matthew 5:45) or those the Lord imposes upon us to prove us (see Abraham 3:25). In addition to the enticements of sin, trials can include doubt, discouragement, and depression. As daunting as these trials can be, God does not test us spiritually beyond our ability to endure. Paul explained, "There hath no temptation taken you but such as is common to man: but God is faithful, who will not suffer you to be tempted [or tested] above that ye are able; but will with the temptation also make a way to escape, that ye may be able to bear it" (1 Corinthians 10:13).

Some who have wandered off and were lost in the mists of darkness may have been saved if they had had a mentor to show them the way. Many of us in the darkness may seek someone to help us. We may talk to our spouse, parent, friend, bishop, or others. We may be disappointed and dismayed if their counsel implies that we have brought our doubts upon ourselves. They may imply we have neglected to nourish our faith and offer us the Primary answers (e.g., read the scriptures, pray, fast) as the solution. Or perhaps they imply we have succumbed to some sin and lost the influence of the Holy Ghost, "for the Spirit of the Lord will not always strive with man" (2 Nephi 26:11). They have been taught that those who follow Christ "shall not walk in darkness, but shall have the light of life" (John 8:12). Therefore, they must conclude we are not following Christ, and the best counsel they can offer us is to repent and come unto Him.

Ostler's survey of those who were experiencing a crisis of faith revealed that:

- 86% believed wholeheartedly in the teachings of the Church;
- 98% held a temple recommend;

---

32. See *Encyclopedia.com*, s.v. "Temptation (In The Bible)," accessed Nov. 8, 2022, https://www.encyclopedia.com/religion/encyclopedias-almanacs-transcripts-and-maps/temptation-bible.

- 98% were keeping the commandments;
- 64% were reading their scriptures daily;
- 82% were having meaningful personal prayer;
- 99% attended church weekly; and
- 79% of those who were endowed attended the temple regularly.[33]

Clearly, the darkness of doubt may come even when we choose to believe and live the gospel. Note what Lehi said: "There *arose* a mist of darkness" (1 Nephi 8:23; emphasis added). Apparently, the people did not cause the darkness through their neglect or disobedience. In fact, they "did come forth, and commence" (1 Nephi 8:22) on the "strait and narrow path which leads to eternal life" (2 Nephi 31:18). The darkness *arose* and overtook them, even though they were on the path. Likewise, the mists of darkness can rise and fall upon us even when we are living the gospel. The dark night of the soul is initiated by a loving Father in Heaven who is transforming us into all we are meant to be.

> *The dark night of the soul is initiated by a loving Father in Heaven who is transforming us into all we are meant to be.*

One who has not experienced the dark night of the soul may not know how to counsel one in the depths of it. A bishop *should* receive divine inspiration and provide perfect counsel to someone in the dark night. But most often, bishops advise those who have weakened their testimonies through their own negligence or choices, and so the Primary answers are most often sufficient to spiritually renew them. Therefore, bishops can fall into the habit of offering a one-size-fits-all solution and may not stop to hear the Spirit whisper, "This circumstance is different and

---

33. David B. Ostler, *Bridges: Ministering to Those Who Question* (Salt Lake City: Greg Kofford Books, 2019), 43.

requires different counsel." As I look back on my service as a bishop, I regretrably recognize there were times I should have stopped and listened more carefully to the Spirit. If I had, I would have provided counsel more suited for those in the depths of the dark night.

COMMUNE WITH THE SPIRIT

As noted previously, in the dark night we may find that the spiritual solutions we learned as children (e.g., read the scriptures, pray, attend church) no longer renew us. To be clear, these disciplines are essential for the nourishment of our testimony in most winters of faith, but in the dark night they may seem futile. The dark night of the soul is an adult challenge for which childhood solutions seem insufficient.

> *The dark night of the soul is an adult challenge for which childhood solutions seem insufficient.*

Wisdom would dictate we should continue to practice the disciplines in the dark night, but the "why bothers" set in as we find the disciplines more discouraging than encouraging. This decreases our faith, increases our doubts, and is contrary to all we have been taught about renewing our faith.

In Lehi's vision of the tree of life, those who found their way through the mists of darkness "caught hold of the end of the rod of iron [which led to the tree]; and they did press forward through the mist of darkness, clinging to the rod of iron, even until they did come forth and partake of the fruit of the tree" (1 Nephi 8:24). This fruit was "the love of God, which sheddeth itself abroad in the hearts of the children of men . . . the most desirable above all things . . . and the most joyous to the soul" (1 Nephi 11:22–23). Nephi explained to his brothers that the iron rod "was the word of God; and whoso would hearken unto the word of God, and would hold fast unto it, they would never perish; neither could the temptations and the fiery darts of the adversary overpower them unto blindness, to lead them away to destruction" (1 Nephi 15:24). We have been taught to "hold to the rod" and promised that it would "guide us through":

> While on our journey here below,
> Beneath temptation's pow'r,
> Through mists of darkness we must go,
> In peril ev'ry hour.
>
> And when temptation's pow'r is nigh,
> Our pathway clouded o'er,
> Upon the rod we can rely,
> And heaven's aid implore.
>
> Hold to the rod, the iron rod;
> 'Tis strong, and bright, and true.
> The iron rod is the word of God;
> 'Twill safely guide us through.[34]

It is true that we can lose our way if we do not hold "fast to the rod of iron" (1 Nephi 8:30). If we neglect to nourish our faith (see Alma 32:38–39) with "the word of God" (1 Nephi 15:24) through prayer, scripture study, church attendance, and so on, our faith can die and we can wander off and become lost. But when the Primary answers no longer work, the "why bothers" may cause us to let the rod slip from our fingers. We may follow the path for a time, keeping the rod of iron within arm's reach, but as the darkness thickens and obscures the path, we may purposely or unwittingly begin to stray from it. The commandments may seem more restraining and sin may seem less serious. Then, before we are aware, we are "[led] away into broad roads . . . and are lost" (1 Nephi 12:17). If we stray too far from the path, we may begin "to kick against the pricks, to persecute the saints, and to fight against God" (Doctrine and Covenants 121:38).

---

34. "The Iron Rod," *Hymns*, no. 174.

It is here in the dark night that the Spirit beckons us to "doubt not, but be believing, and begin as in times of old, and come unto the Lord with all your heart, and work out your own salvation with fear and trembling before him" (Mormon 9:27).

In the mists of the thick darkness, how do we begin to "come unto the Lord" (Mormon 9:27)? We must find alternative ways to commune with the Spirit until the darkness parts enough for us to find the path. These alternative methods would normally be insufficient to spiritually sustain us, but when our spirit is starving, these morsels are manna to the soul.

In the dark night, each of us must find a way to commune with the Spirit; that is, to choose an activity that gives us a taste of the fruit of the Spirit. Paul taught, "But the fruit of the Spirit is love, joy, peace, longsuffering, gentleness, goodness, faith, meekness, temperance" (Galatians 5:22–23). "For the fruit of the Spirit is in all goodness and righteousness and truth; Proving what is acceptable unto the Lord" (Ephesians 5:9–10).

Note that Paul speaks of a singular fruit but lists what seem to be multiple fruits. This may be due to an error in punctuation. One Bible commentator suggests that "another way to punctuate this is 'love' followed by a colon."[35] Interpreted this way, the fruit of the Spirit is love, and the other feelings—joy, peace, longsuffering, and so on— are all attributes of love.

In the dark night, we must seek to feel our Savior's and heavenly parents' love for us. We may experience it through any of the attributes, though peace is preeminent. The Lord said to Oliver Cowdery, "Cast your mind upon the night that you cried unto me in your heart, that you might know concerning the truth of these things. Did I not speak

---

35. "Galatians 5:22," Bible Gateway, accessed Nov. 10, 2022, https://www.biblegateway.com/passage/?search=Galatians%205%3A22&version=NET.

peace to your mind concerning the matter? What greater witness can you have than from God?" (Doctrine and Covenants 6:22–23).

Why is peace the greatest witness? Some have said that peace is a witness from the Holy Spirit that is impossible for the adversary to counterfeit.[36] Therefore, it may be the most trusted emotion.

In the dark night, we must seek peace by communing with the Spirit. What works for one person may be distasteful for another; therefore, we must "work out [our] own salvation" (Mormon 9:27). To be clear, to "work out [our] own salvation" is not an excuse to leave the path, as we may want to do in the dark night. However, if we have left the path, we are to "work out [our] own salvation" to return to it.

Some commune with the Spirit in nature: walking in the woods, sitting by the ocean, hiking in the mountains, and so on. Some do so through music. One person, in her dark night, began to listen to Christian music in her car. It was mainstream Christian music that some Latter-day Saints would find irreverent, but it helped her commune with the Spirit. Some commune with the Spirit by serving others. Some may read books or listen to podcasts that help them feel the Spirit. There are many activities we can do to commune with the Spirit, and each person must learn what works for them.

Any act that turns our thoughts to God, no matter how seemingly insignificant, will invoke the Holy Spirit and the aid of angels. We may not see them, feel them, or even sense that our small act is having an effect, but little by little our spirit is renewed until we again desire to reach for the rod of iron.

As noted earlier, communing with the Spirit in the dark night is like eating during an illness. An illness can cause us to lose our appetite. We may not want to eat while we are sick, but as we begin to recover, we might eat something bland to see if we can hold it down.

---

36. Brian K. Ashton, "Three Lessons on Love, Joy, and Peace," *Liahona*, Apr. 2019, 27.

Then we eat a little more . . . and a little more. Our appetite gradually returns as we get better. Then, as we continue to eat, we become stronger and recover.

These simple activities of communing with the Spirit are the bland bites in the illness of the dark night. Though they are not sufficient to spiritually sustain us, they strengthen us and help us recover until our appetite for the word of God returns. Then, just as we want a hearty meal when we are fully recovered from an illness, we will desire to "feast upon the words of Christ" (2 Nephi 32:3) as we emerge from the dark night. We can then seize the rod of iron and press forward on the path.

> *Any act that turns our thoughts to God, no matter how seemingly insignificant, will invoke the Holy Spirit and the aid of angels.*

BE HUMBLE

Alma asked the people of Zarahemla, "Behold, are ye stripped of pride? I say unto you, if ye are not ye are not prepared to meet God. Behold ye must prepare quickly; for the kingdom of heaven is soon at hand, and such an one hath not eternal life" (Alma 5:28).

In the dark night, we are stripped of pride and "compelled to be humble" (Alma 32:16). The self-confidence we gained from our success in the Young Adult stage of faith is replaced with self-loathing. We, like Nephi and Paul, declare, "O wretched man that I am!" (2 Nephi 4:17; Romans 7:24).

"Moses was caught up into an exceedingly high mountain, and he saw God face to face, and he talked with him, and the glory of God was upon [him]" (Moses 1:1–2). He was then shown a vision of "the world and the ends thereof, and all the children of men which are, and which were created" (Moses 1:8). "And the presence of God withdrew from Moses, that his glory was not upon Moses; and Moses was left unto himself. And as he was left unto himself, he fell unto the earth. And . . . he said unto himself: Now, for this cause I know that man is nothing, which thing I never had supposed" (Moses 1:9–10).

Though Moses was not experiencing the dark night of the soul, his description of his experience bears resemblance to how some describe the dark night. We feel God's presence has withdrawn, we feel the warmth of His glory no longer shines upon us, we feel alone, and we become acutely aware that "man is nothing."

King Benjamin taught:

> Men drink damnation to their own souls except they humble themselves and become as little children, and believe that salvation was, and is, and is to come, in and through the atoning blood of Christ, the Lord Omnipotent.
>
> For the natural man is an enemy to God, and has been from the fall of Adam, and will be, forever and ever, unless he yields to the enticings of the Holy Spirit, and putteth off the natural man and becometh a saint through the atonement of Christ the Lord, and becometh as a child, submissive, meek, humble, patient, full of love, willing to submit to all things which the Lord seeth fit to inflict upon him, even as a child doth submit to his father. (Mosiah 3:18–19)

The "natural man" causes us to be "an enemy to God" because it wages "war against the soul" (1 Peter 2:11), "for the flesh lusteth against the Spirit, and the Spirit against the flesh" (Galatians 5:17). In the dark night, our Father in Heaven helps us shed "the natural man" so we can become "as a child, submissive, meek, humble, patient, full of love, willing to submit to all things which the Lord seeth fit to inflict upon him, even as a child doth submit to his father" (Mosiah 3:19).

We must be stripped of pride because pride pits us in opposition to God and causes us to defy His will. President Ezra Taft Benson taught:

The central feature of pride is enmity—enmity toward God and enmity toward our fellowmen. Enmity means "hatred toward, hostility to, or a state of opposition." It is the power by which Satan wishes to reign over us.

Pride is essentially competitive in nature. We pit our will against God's. When we direct our pride toward God, it is in the spirit of "my will and not thine be done." As Paul said, they "seek their own, not the things which are Jesus Christ's." (Philip. 2:21.)

Our will in competition to God's will allows desires, appetites, and passions to go unbridled. (See Alma 38:12; 3 Ne. 12:30.)

The proud cannot accept the authority of God giving direction to their lives. (See Hel. 12:6.) They pit their perceptions of truth against God's great knowledge, their abilities versus God's priesthood power, their accomplishments against His mighty works.

Our enmity toward God takes on many labels, such as rebellion, hard-heartedness, stiff-neckedness, unrepentant, puffed up, easily offended, and sign seekers. The proud wish God would agree with them. They aren't interested in changing their opinions to agree with God's.

Another major portion of this very prevalent sin of pride is enmity toward our fellowmen. We are tempted daily to elevate ourselves above others and diminish them. (See Hel. 6:17; Doctrine and Covenants 58:41.)

The proud make every man their adversary by pitting their intellects, opinions, works, wealth, talents, or any other worldly measuring device against others. In the words of C. S. Lewis: "Pride gets no pleasure out of having something, only out of having more of it than the next man. . . . It is the comparison that makes you proud: the pleasure of being above the rest. Once the element of competition has gone, pride has gone." (*Mere Christianity,* New York: Macmillan, 1952, pp. 109–10.) [37]

In the dark night, we are "stripped of pride" (Alma 5:28) and feel like we are "nothing" (Moses 1:10). We may attempt to bolster our

---

37. Ezra Taft Benson, "Beware of Pride," *Ensign,* May 1989, 4.

pride by finding fault in others. Unable to lift ourselves, we tear down those around us in our thoughts or in gossip. Cutting them down helps us feel a little taller.

We most often find fault in our Church leaders. As was noted earlier, finding fault is the first sign of failing faith.[38] For this reason, the Lord protects us from fault-finding through our temple covenants. In the temple, we covenant to avoid "evil speaking of the Lord's anointed." Before we enter the temple, and each time we renew our temple recommend, we answer these questions:

- Do you sustain the President of The Church of Jesus Christ of Latter-day Saints as the prophet, seer, and revelator and as the only person on the earth authorized to exercise all priesthood keys?
- Do you sustain the members of the First Presidency and the Quorum of the Twelve Apostles as prophets, seers, and revelators?
- Do you sustain the other General Authorities and local leaders of the Church?[39]

To sustain means to "support, hold, or bear up from below; bear the weight of, as a structure" and "to keep [one] from giving way, as under trial or affliction."[40] Sustaining one who is called to serve in the Church means much more than raising our hand for the sustaining vote to signal our agreement with their calling. Sustaining means to do all we can do to bear them up to prevent them from giving up under the burden of their responsibilities. When we raise our hand in

38. *Teachings of Presidents of the Church: Joseph Smith* (2007), 318.

39. "Church Updates Temple Recommend Interview Questions" (Oct. 6, 2019), newsroom.ChurchofJesusChrist.org.

40. *Dictionary.com*, s.v. "Sustain," accessed Nov. 7, 2022, https://www.dictionary.com/browse/sustain.

a sustaining vote, we are essentially covenanting with them, and God, that we will do all we can to ensure they do not fail.

I was thirty-one years old the first time I was called to serve as a bishop. I was young, inexperienced, and immature and felt wholly inadequate when measured against the responsibilities of that calling. A week after I was sustained in sacrament meeting, I was entering the chapel to watch a session of general conference. I was burdened by the responsibilities of my calling and my head was down. As I entered the chapel, I almost bumped into the chest of Ron Mikesell, who was a giant both physically and spiritually.

He stood in front of me, looked down at me, and said in a gruff but gentle voice, "Bishop, I wasn't here when you were sustained last Sunday. But I want you to know . . ." He then raised his hand to the square and said resolutely, "I sustain you."

In that moment, the burden felt a little lighter and I felt a little more confident because I knew Brother Mikesell supported me. I am forever grateful for his sustaining vote and the lesson he taught me about the importance of sustaining the leaders of the Church.

In the dark night, we must be humble and allow ourselves to be stripped of pride so we can submit fully to the will of God.

Accept Ourselves

The final practice for enduring the dark night is to learn to accept ourselves. In the Young Adult stage, we strive to fulfill our Esteem and Self-Actualization needs and press forward to become the person we want to be. We are proud of our successes, grateful for our talents, and confident in our ability to fulfill our ambitions and achieve our goals. We believe our weaknesses are actually strengths in infancy, and failures are merely learning opportunities. Everything we do is about pressing forward to become all we want to be.

Paul taught that we see ourselves "through a glass, darkly" (1 Corinthians 13:12). In other words, the image we see in the mirror is obscured. Mirrors in Paul's time were made of metal, often brass. The metal had to be frequently polished with a sponge and powdered pumice.[41] An unpolished mirror reflected a dark, obscured, imperfect image. When we look at ourselves in the mirror in the Young Adult stage, our image is obscured by our self-confidence and self-consciousness, but in the dark night, "we see face to face" (1 Corinthians 13:12). We are stripped of our facade and come face to face with who we really are, and we don't like what we see.

We discover that the Lord's image is not "engraven upon [our] countenances" (Alma 5:19) as we once thought. We see all that we are, and all that we aren't, and we admit that our Christlike behavior is a pretense. Our sins, lusts, insecurities, imperfections, envies, jealousies, strife, selfishness, anger, and haughtiness—all that is ugly about us— is accentuated in the dark night's unmercifully polished mirror, and it mars our image like hairy moles, scars, wrinkles, and blemishes. We see that all the sacrifices we have made in the service of God amount to little, for "if [we] should serve him with all [our] whole souls yet [we] would be unprofitable servants" (Mosiah 2:21).

This unfiltered view of ourselves should not surprise us, for the Lord said, "If men come unto me I will show unto them their weakness. I give unto men weakness that they may be humble; and my grace is sufficient for all men that humble themselves before me" (Ether 12:27).

Then, in the depths of our self-loathing, something wonderful begins to happen. We begin to accept ourselves. We accept who we are with all our ugliness. We must not excuse our weaknesses or

---

41. See "What Does 'Now, We See Through a Glass Darkly' Mean?", Then Face to Face, accessed Nov. 7, 2022, https://thenface2face.wordpress.com/ what-does-now-we-see-through-a-glass-darkly-mean/.

wickedness or feel less desire to forsake all ungodliness (see Moroni 10:32), but we *should* simply accept who we are instead of trying so desperately to be who we are not. We realize the Lord commanded us to "be ye therefore perfect" (Matthew 5:48), but He did not say, "Be ye therefore perfect now!"

Elder Jeffrey R. Holland taught:

> As children of God, we should not demean or vilify ourselves, as if beating up on ourselves is somehow going to make us the person God wants us to become. No! With a willingness to repent and a desire for increased righteousness always in our hearts, I would hope we could pursue personal improvement in a way that doesn't include getting ulcers or anorexia, feeling depressed or demolishing our self-esteem. That is not what the Lord wants for Primary children or anyone else who honestly sings, "I'm trying to be like Jesus."[42]

Nephi taught that "it is by grace that we are saved, after all we can do" (2 Nephi 25:23). In the Adolescent and Young Adult stages of faith, we act as though we are saved by "all we can do," aided by the grace of Christ. We sometimes forget we are saved by grace . . . period. In fact, everyone who does not commit the unpardonable sin of blasphemy against the Holy Ghost is saved in the kingdom of heaven. Joseph Smith taught that the Savior "saves all the works of his hands, except those sons of perdition who deny the Son after the Father has revealed him. Wherefore, he saves all except them" (Doctrine and Covenants 76:43–44). Brigham Young declared, "Every person who does not sin away the day of grace, and become an angel to the Devil, will be brought forth to inherit a kingdom of glory."[43] All but the sons of perdition are saved solely by the grace of Christ to dwell in the celestial, terrestrial, or the telestial kingdom. There is nothing we can do

---

42. Jeffrey R. Holland, "Be Ye Therefore Perfect—Eventually," *Ensign* or *Liahona*, Nov. 2017, 40.

43. *Teachings of Presidents of the Church: Brigham Young* (1997), 288.

to save ourselves; "all we can do" is choose the *degree* of our salvation through obedience. In the dark night, we understand that "[we] have not come thus far save it were by the word of Christ with unshaken faith in him," and we must rely "wholly upon the merits of him who is mighty to save" (2 Nephi 31:19).

Additionally, we begin to see perfection even in our imperfections. We recognize that "God hath chosen the weak things of the world" (1 Corinthians 1:27) and has used our weakness to demonstrate His wisdom (see Doctrine and Covenants 1:24). Consider the following story as an example of this.

> A man in India had two large pots, each hung on each end of a pole which he carried across his neck. One of the pots had a crack in it, and while the other pot was perfect and always delivered a full portion of water at the end of the long walk from the stream to his house, the cracked pot arrived only half full.
>
> For a full two years, this went on daily, with the man delivering only one and a half pots full of water to his house. Of course, the perfect pot was proud of its accomplishments, perfect to the end for which it was made. But the poor cracked pot was ashamed of its own imperfection and miserable that it was able to accomplish only half of what it had been made to do.
>
> After two years of what it perceived to be a bitter failure, it spoke to the water bearer one day by the stream and said, "I am ashamed of myself, and I want to apologize to you."
>
> The man asked, "Why? What are you ashamed of?"
>
> The Pot replied, "For these past two years I am able to deliver only half of my load because this crack in my side causes water to leak out all the way back to your house. Because of my flaws, you don't get full value for your efforts."
>
> The man felt sorry for the old cracked pot, and in his compassion, he said, "As we return to the house, I want you to notice the beautiful flowers along the path." As they went up the hill, the old cracked pot took notice of the sun warming the beautiful wild flowers on the side of the path, and this cheered it somewhat. But at

the end of the trail, it still felt bad because it had leaked out half its load, and so again it apologized to the man for its failure.

The bearer said to the pot, "Did you notice that there were flowers only on your side of your path, but not on the other pot's side? That's because I have always known about your flaw, and I took advantage of it. I planted flower seeds on your side of the path, and every day while we walk back from the stream, you've watered them. For two years I have been able to pick these beautiful flowers to decorate my table. Without you being just the way you are, we would not have these beautiful flowers to grace our house."[44]

In the dark night, we can accept ourselves. We can embrace our brokenness and see how our Father in Heaven has perfectly used our imperfections to bless those around us. Then, through His grace, He can make "our weak things become strong" (Ether 12:27).

Redefining our Relationship with God

As dawn approaches and we sense we may soon emerge from the dark night, we learn to redefine our relationship with God. We learn to see Him from new perspectives and connect with Him in new ways. If in the past we saw Him as jealous (see Exodus 20:5) and vengeful (see Romans 1:19), as the dawn approaches, we begin to comprehend His infinite grace and mercy. If we saw Him as cold and heartless for allowing evil to afflict the innocent, we begin to sense the depths of His infinite love (see John 3:16) and compassion (see Alma 7:11–12), and we see the wisdom of agency (see 2 Nephi 2:11–16). If we saw Him as disinterested in our calamities, we begin to see His hand orchestrating the trials that purify us.

Malachi taught, "He is like a refiner's fire, and like fullers' soap: And he shall sit as a refiner and purifier of silver: and he shall purify

---

44. "The Cracked Pot," Moral Stories, accessed Nov. 10, 2022, https://www.moralstories.org/the-cracked-pot/.

the sons of Levi, and purge them as gold and silver" (Malachi 3:2). The Lord said, "And I will bring [them] through the fire, and will refine them as silver is refined, and will try them as gold is tried: they shall call on my name, and I will hear them: I will say, It is my people: and they shall say, The Lord is my God" (Zechariah 13:9). "Behold, I have refined thee, but not with silver; I have chosen thee in the furnace of affliction" (Isaiah 48:10).

Greek scholar Kenneth Wuest penned this beautiful description of God's refining fire:

> The picture here is of an ancient goldsmith who puts his crude gold ore in a crucible, subjects it to intense heat, and thus liquefies the mass. The impurities rise to the surface and are skimmed off. When the metalworker is able to see the reflection of his face clearly mirrored in the surface of the liquid, he takes it off the fire, for he knows that the contents are pure gold. So it is with God and His child. He puts us in the crucible of Christian suffering, in which process sin is gradually put out of our lives, our faith is purified from the slag of unbelief that somehow mingles with it so often, and the result is the reflection of the face of Jesus Christ in the character of the Christian. This, above all, God the Father desires to see. Christlikeness is God's ideal for His child. Christian suffering is one of the most potent means to that end.[45]

The purification process of heating and skimming seems gentle and gradual. Perhaps this has not been the experience for some of us. For some of us, God's purification process is more blacksmith than goldsmith. For example, to forge a sword, the blacksmith heats the metal to nearly melting. He beats it with a hammer and then heats it and beats it again. He repeats the heat and beat process until it takes the shape he desires. He then lets it cool. Grinds it. Reheats it.

---

45. Paul Tautges, "The Refiner's Fire," Association of Certified Biblical Counselors, Sept. 18, 2020, https://biblicalcounseling.com/resource-library/articles/the-refiners-fire/.

Quenches it in order to harden and temper it. Then he grinds and grinds until it is polished.[46]

Whether our imperfections are gently skimmed from us or beaten out of us, the result is the same. We are purified and perfected in Christ (see Moroni 10:32–33).

Peter taught that this purification of our faith is more precious than gold. He said, "That the trial of your faith, being much more precious than of gold that perisheth, though it be tried with fire, might be found unto praise and honour and glory at the appearing of Jesus Christ: Whom having not seen, ye love; in whom, though now ye see him not, yet believing, ye rejoice with joy unspeakable and full of glory: Receiving the end of your faith, even the salvation of your souls" (1 Peter 1:7–9).

I once introduced a coworker to the gospel. His conversion was swift and miraculous. A few weeks after his baptism, he came to speak with me. He sat in the chair across from me and leaned forward with his elbows on his thighs, hands clasped. There was excitement in his voice as he exclaimed, "I finally understand!" He said it with such fervency that I thought he had unlocked all the mysteries of the universe. And he had. He then said with emphasis and finality, "God . . . is . . . my . . . Father." He then leaned back, mouth open, head cocked, half smiling in awe as he realized that one statement answered every important question about life.

As we redefine our relationship with God near the end of the dark night, we come to the same extraordinary conclusion: God . . . is . . . our . . . Father. When we understand that He is a perfect, loving Father, we know we can trust in Him. We can submit ourselves to His will and know that His gentle hand is guiding our lives for our ultimate benefit.

---

46. "How to Forge a Sword: A Step-By-Step Guide," Blacksmith Code, Jan. 8, 2021, https://blacksmithcode.com/how-to-make-a-sword/.

Paul declared, "And because ye are sons, God hath sent forth the Spirit of his Son into your hearts, crying, Abba, Father. Wherefore thou art no more a servant, but a son; and if a son, then an heir of God through Christ" (Galatians 4:6–7).

Don J. Black, in his talk titled "Hand to Hand Combat with Satan," shared an experience he once had on a flight. He was sitting near a Jewish man and his young son, who was on a plane for the first time. As the plane took off, the young boy excitedly pointed out the window and said, "Abba! Abba! Look! Look, Abba!" In that moment, Don concluded that *Abba* is not the formal, impersonal title for father; it is an informal, personal title like *daddy* or *papa*.

When an adult refers to their father as Abba, it conveys the highest respect,[47] obedience, and submissiveness.[48] Hence, when Jesus was in Gethsemane, He addressed his Father as Abba as He pleaded, "Take away this cup from me" and then submitted with the words, "Nevertheless not what I will, but what thou wilt" (Mark 14:36).

As we redefine our relationship with God, we are more willing to obey Him and submit to His will. Like the Savior in Gethsemane, God becomes to us more like the personal Abba than the impersonal Father (see Galatians 4:6–7).

Conclusion

The dark night of the soul is a personalized chrysalis that transforms us from what we thought we wanted to be into what our Father knows we will want to be. It is a "refiner's fire" (Malachi 3:2) and

47. "Calling God 'Abba, Father'," Theology of Work, accessed Nov. 8, 2022, https://www.theologyofwork.org/the-high-calling/daily-reflection/calling-god-abba-father-1.

48. Chad Harrington, "The Biblical Meaning of 'Abba,' and It's Not Daddy," HIM Publications, accessed Nov. 8, 2022, https://himpublications.com/blog/meaning-abba/.

"furnace of affliction" (Isaiah 48:10) that purifies and sanctifies us, turning our selfishness into selflessness and our prideful ambition into humble submission.

Many in the dark night lose their way, wander off, and are lost (see 1 Nephi 8:23). Those who "press forward through the mist of darkness" (1 Nephi 8:24) are eventually enveloped in "the love of God, which sheddeth itself abroad in the hearts of the children of men . . . [and is] the most desirable above all things . . . and the most joyous to the soul" (1 Nephi 11:22–23).

> *The dark night of the soul is a personalized chrysalis that transforms us from what we thought we wanted to be into what our Father knows we will want to be.*

Key Point Summary

- The dark night of the soul is a preeminent transformational experience.
- Symptoms of the dark night include profound doubt and feeling the absence of God.
- The dark night of the soul is the deconstruction of faith that leaves us hopeless.
- The dark night is a transition to greater faith.
- There are seven recommended practices for enduring the dark night:
    o Redefine the crisis
    o Surrender to the will of God
    o Shed selfishness
    o Seek a mentor
    o Commune with the Spirit
    o Be humble
    o Accept ourselves

7

THE ADULT STAGE OF FAITH

"When your will is God's will, you will have your will."

—Charles Spurgeon[1]

We consider someone an adult when they reach a defined age of maturity (e.g., eighteen years old). As noted earlier, the dark night of the soul often occurs between the ages of thirty and fifty. Therefore, many of us experience the Adult stage of faith, which follows the dark night, as older adults. Hence, for many there is a disparity in age between the adult stage of human development and the Adult stage of faith. For the purposes of this book, the adult stage of human development is defined less by one's age and more by one's ability to reflect on their experiences and apply wisdom.

At this stage in human development, we have established ourselves in our chosen profession. Our associates at work and in the community value our knowledge and experience and some see us as a mentor. If we have children, they are busy with school and extracurricular

---

1. Charles Spurgeon, "When your will," AZ Quotes, accessed Nov. 9, 2022, https://www.azquotes.com/quote/360557.

activities. Perhaps some of our older kids are entering college or starting their own careers. If we are married, our relationship with our spouse is more tightly woven than it has ever been or tattered by the storms in the dark night. If unmarried, we may be actively seeking a spouse or content being single.

It is a bittersweet time. We are mindful of our accomplishments and mournful for our unfulfilled hopes and dreams. We appreciate our efforts that secured the success we now enjoy and regret the lack of effort that could have secured greater success. At this stage, success is measured less by what we have and more by what we hoped to become. For example, being a respected parent means more than fame and fortune.

We have developed wisdom through our years of experience. Wisdom is applied knowledge. Journalist and humorist Miles Kingston once said, "Knowledge is knowing that a tomato is a fruit. Wisdom is not putting it in a fruit salad."[2] The scriptures state that "wisdom is better than rubies" (Proverbs 8:11), "strength" (Ecclesiastes 9:16), and "weapons of war" (Ecclesiastes 9:18). At the adult stage of life, our experience gives us wisdom.

Similarly, in the Adult stage of faith, we apply the wisdom we have gained through the previous stages of faith and the dark night of the soul. As we emerge from the dark night, we see life, others, and the Savior through a new lens that forever changes our perspective of who we are and who we are meant to be.

Emerging from the Dark Night

Consider Alma's words to the people of Zarahemla. His description of the converted who escaped the oppression of King Noah to

---

2. Philip Sheldrake, *The Business of Influence: Reframing Marketing and PR for the Digital Age* (Chichester, England: Wiley, 2011), 153.

join the church in the land of Mormon could also be applied to those who are emerging from the dark night:

> Behold, he changed their hearts; yea, he awakened them out of a deep sleep, and they awoke unto God. Behold, they were in the midst of darkness; nevertheless, their souls were illuminated by the light of the everlasting word; yea, they were encircled about by the bands of death, and the chains of hell, and an everlasting destruction did await them.
>
> And now I ask of you, my brethren, were they destroyed? Behold, I say unto you, Nay, they were not.
>
> And again I ask, were the bands of death broken, and the chains of hell which encircled them about, were they loosed? I say unto you, Yea, they were loosed, and their souls did expand, and they did sing redeeming love. And I say unto you that they are saved. (Alma 5:7–9)

Alma explains that the people were in the "midst of darkness," and as they emerged, "their souls did expand." As noted earlier, Alma elaborated on the expansion of the soul in his lecture on faith to the Zoramites. He explained that the enlargement of the soul is evidence that our faith is becoming a perfect knowledge.

> If it be a true seed, or a good seed, if ye do not cast it out by your unbelief, that ye will resist the Spirit of the Lord, behold, it will begin to swell within your breasts; and when you feel these swelling motions, ye will begin to say within yourselves—It must needs be that this is a good seed, or that the word is good, for it beginneth to enlarge my soul; yea, it beginneth to enlighten my understanding, yea, it beginneth to be delicious to me.
>
> And now, behold, is your knowledge perfect? Yea, your knowledge is perfect in that thing, and your faith is dormant; and this because you know, for ye know that the word hath swelled your souls, and ye also know that it hath sprouted up, that your understanding doth begin to be enlightened, and your mind doth begin to expand.

O then, is not this real? I say unto you, Yea, because it is light;
and whatsoever is light, is good, because it is discernible, therefore
ye must know that it is good. (Alma 32:28, 34–35)

As we emerge from the dark night, our "understanding doth begin to be enlightened." Notice the words "doth begin." For many,
emerging from the dark night is a gradual process that occurs over
time, not an instantaneous event.

One Saturday, I needed to stop by my office to pick something
up. I took my young daughter, Bethany, with me. No one was in the
building, so all of the lights were off. The only light in the building
emanated from the dim exit signs over the exterior doors. The building was a maze of cubicles, but I walked the path to my office multiple
times each work day, so I knew the way well.

As the door closed behind us, shutting out the light from the
morning sun, we were engulfed in near darkness. My daughter looked
up at me and asked, "Daddy, can we please turn on the lights?"

I considered turning on the lights, but then I thought to myself,
This is a perfect opportunity to teach her the principle of faith. I looked
down at her and said, "Bethany, take my hand and I will show you
the way."

With trust in her eyes, she put her hand in mine, and I led her . . .
directly into a post.

Apparently, her collision with the post was painful because she
started crying. So, I turned on the lights and tried to comfort her. The
Spirit then whispered to me, "Trust in the *Lord* with all thine heart;
and lean not unto thine own understanding. In all thy ways acknowledge him, and *he* shall direct thy paths" (Proverbs 3:5–6; emphasis
added).

In the dark night, we may beg, as my daughter did, "Father, can
you please just turn on the lights?" But He doesn't. Instead, He says to
us, "Take my hand and I will show you the way." Unlike me, He is a

perfect Father, and He promises, "I will bring the blind by a way that they knew not; I will lead them in paths that they have not known: I will make darkness light before them, and crooked things straight. These things will I do unto them, and not forsake them" (Isaiah 42:16).

Once He has led us through the darkness and we sense that we are soon to emerge from it, He does not normally flip a light switch and dispel all of our doubts at once. Instead, as Alma explained, our understanding "doth begin to be enlightened" (Alma 32:34). Elder David A. Bednar taught that answers sometimes come instantaneously, like turning on a light in a dark room, but more often they come gradually like the sunrise. He said:

> In contrast to turning on a light in a dark room, the light from the rising sun did not immediately burst forth. Rather, gradually and steadily the intensity of the light increased, and the darkness of night was replaced by the radiance of morning. Eventually, the sun did dawn over the skyline. But the visual evidence of the sun's impending arrival was apparent hours before the sun actually appeared over the horizon. This experience was characterized by subtle and gradual discernment of light. . . .
>
> The gradual increase of light radiating from the rising sun is like receiving a message from God "line upon line, precept upon precept" (2 Nephi 28:30). Most frequently, revelation comes in small increments over time and is granted according to our desire, worthiness, and preparation. Such communications from Heavenly Father gradually and gently "distil upon [our souls] as the dews from heaven" (Doctrine and Covenants 121:45). This pattern of revelation tends to be more common than rare.[3]

Similarly, the Lord explained, "That which is of God is light; and he that receiveth light"—including the light of testimony (see Alma 32:35)—"and continueth in God, receiveth more light; and that light

---

3. David A. Bednar, "The Spirit of Revelation," *Ensign* or *Liahona*, May 2011, 87.

groweth brighter and brighter until the perfect day" (Doctrine and Covenants 50:24).

Emerging from the dark night is a process of receiving a little light, continuing in that light, receiving a little more light, and allowing the light to gradually grow brighter and brighter until our knowledge is perfect. "For behold, thus saith the Lord God: I will give unto the children of men line upon line, precept upon precept, here a little and there a little; and blessed are those who hearken unto my precepts, and lend an ear unto my counsel, for they shall learn wisdom; for unto him that receiveth I will give more" (2 Nephi 28:30).

As we follow this pattern of receiving a little light, then a little more, and then a little more, the light of the Spirit gradually dispels our doubts until we "chase darkness from among [us]" (Doctrine and Covenants 50:25).

President Joseph F. Smith explained how this pattern dispelled his own doubts:

> As a boy . . . I would frequently . . . ask the Lord to show me some marvelous thing, in order that I might receive a testimony. But the Lord withheld marvels from me, and showed me the truth, line upon line . . . until He made me to know the truth from the crown of my head to the soles of my feet, and until doubt and fear had been absolutely purged from me. He did not have to send an angel from the heavens to do this, nor did He have to speak with the trump of an archangel. By the whisperings of the still small voice of the Spirit of the living God, He gave to me the testimony I possess. And by this principle and power He will give to all the children of men a knowledge of the truth that will stay with them, and it will make them to know the truth, as God knows it, and to do the will of the Father as Christ does it. And no amount of marvelous manifestations will ever accomplish this.[4]

---

4. Joseph F. Smith, in Conference Report, Apr. 1900, 40–41.

The hallmark of the Adult stage of faith is a "mighty change of heart" (Alma 5:12). This mighty change includes two phases—what some have called the journey inward and the journey outward.[5]

The Journey Inward

The journey inward is discovering who we really are and what we are meant to be. It begins in the dark night as we redefine the crisis, surrender to the will of God, shed our selfishness, counsel with mentors, commune with the Spirit, become more humble, and learn to accept ourselves.[6] The journey inward continues as we emerge from the dark night.

When I was a full-time missionary in Harrisburg, Illinois, a tornado ripped through one of the towns in our area during the night. The next morning, my companion and I went to the town to check on a family in our ward. Fortunately, their house suffered only minor damage, but many of their neighbors' homes were piles of rubble. The residents of those homes, who were still in shock, were precariously balancing on the debris with unsteady legs as they picked through the rubble to find valuables. They were unconcerned about those things that were expensive, but they were greatly concerned about those things that were irreplaceable: pictures, heirlooms, and memories they hoped to rescue and preserve.

As we emerge from the dark night, the sun's light begins to enlighten our minds. As the darkness dissipates, we begin to see the damage done by the adversary's "mighty winds, yea, his shafts in the whirlwind" (Helaman 5:12). We see that our life is a pile of debris. The journey inward is like picking through the rubble for what is most

---

5. Janet O. Hagberg and Robert A. Guelich, *The Critical Journey: Stages in the Life of Faith* (Salem, WI: Sheffield Publishing Company, 2005), 91, 113.

6. See chapter 6.

valuable. We see how we have wounded others. We sense the serious-ness of our sins and how they have wounded us. We stand unsteady as we consider how lost we were in the "dark and dreary waste" (1 Nephi 8:7), and we pick through the rubble of our lives seeking to recover those things that are most precious and irreplaceable: relationships, our self-worth, and communion with God.

It is here that we begin to draw from the wisdom of our life experi-ence. As we do, we feel regret, "for in much wisdom is much grief: and he that increaseth knowledge increaseth sorrow" (Ecclesiastes 1:18). We look back and see the things in our lives that we thought were paramount but in retrospect were frivolous. We see "all the works that [we have] done under the sun; and, behold, all is vanity and vexation of spirit" (Ecclesiastes 1:14). We acknowledge where we have wasted time, energy, and resources laying up for ourselves "treasures upon earth" (Matthew 6:19) to "gratify our pride, [and] our vain ambition" (Doctrine and Covenants 121:37).

We consider how much of our lives we have vainly spent on selfish pursuits, and we acknowledge that our efforts have not yielded true and lasting happiness. This knowledge of our past gives us wisdom for our future, and we begin to think there may be something more. Perhaps our Father has a different plan for us. Perhaps we, like Saul, have been "kick[ing] against the pricks" (Acts 9:5) and it is now time for us to "submit cheerfully and with patience to all the will of the Lord" (Mosiah 24:15).

Gradually, our appetite for the things of the soul returns, and we begin to "hunger and thirst after righteousness" (Matthew 5:6). Prayer, scripture study, church attendance—all the Primary an-swers—begin "to be delicious" (Alma 32:28) to us, and we desire to "feast upon the words of Christ" (2 Nephi 32:3) just as we did in the Adolescent and Young Adult stages. The difference is the motive. In the Adolescent stage, we studied the scriptures because we were ashamed of our ignorance and wanted to build our Esteem. In the Young Adult stage, we studied the scriptures because we know the Lord will come as a thief in the night (see Luke 12:39), and "blessed is that servant, whom his lord when he cometh shall find so doing" (Luke 12:43–44). In the Adult stage, scripture study, prayer, and the other disciplines are a salve for the wounded soul and create quiet communion with God.

In communion with God, we seek direction from Him. In the past, we most often prayed that He would direct us to know how to do what *we* wanted to do. Now we pray that He will direct us to know what *He* wants us to do. "Prayer is the act by which the will of the Father and the will of the child are brought into correspondence with each other. . . . We pray in Christ's name when our mind is the mind of Christ, and our wishes the wishes of Christ—when His words abide in us" (Bible Dictionary, "Prayer").

Alma, speaking of those who believed the words of Abinadi, explained, "A mighty change was also wrought in their hearts, and they humbled themselves and put their trust in the true and living God. And behold, they were faithful until the end" (Alma 5:13). A similar mighty change takes place in us during our journey inward. In essence, we experience a second conversion as we rediscover God. Our relationship with Him becomes more intimate, and we commune with Him at a deeper level than we did in the past. He begins to heal our deep, unresolved spiritual and psychological wounds. He restores our soul (see Psalm 23:3).

During our journey inward, we ask more questions. Our questions may cause others to believe that our doubts still shake our faith. However, our questions during the journey inward stem from a sincere desire to understand truth, whereas in the previous stages, we often questioned to justify our doubts.

During the journey inward, we relinquish our ego. Perhaps for the first time in our lives, we feel we can lay upon the altar all of our "vain ambition" (Doctrine and Covenants 121:37), and "with an eye single to the glory of God" (Doctrine and Covenants 4:5), we can consecrate all of our time, talents, and everything with which the Lord has blessed us for the building up of the kingdom of God on the earth and for the establishment of Zion. "Obedience ceases to be an irritant and becomes our quest."[7] We desire to "[put] off the natural man and [become] a saint through the atonement of Christ the Lord" (Mosiah 3:16).

We humble ourselves and trust He has a unique purpose for us just as the water bearer had for the cracked pot. We believe He will reveal that unique purpose, and we are willing to commit ourselves to it. As it says in the hymn "I'll Go Where You Want Me to Go":

> So trusting my all to thy tender care,
> And knowing thou lovest me,
> I'll do thy will with a heart sincere:
> I'll be what you want me to be.[8]

During our journey inward, God reveals who He wants us to be. We discover the unique purpose for which we were "foreordained before the foundation of the world" (1 Peter 1:20). As Paul states:

> We know that all things work together for good to them that love God, to them who are the called according to his purpose.
>
> For whom he did foreknow, he also did predestinate to be conformed to the image of his Son, that he might be the firstborn among many brethren.
>
> Moreover whom he did predestinate, them he also called: and whom he called, them he also justified: and whom he justified, them he also glorified. (Romans 8:28–30)

---

7. Ezra Taft Benson, quoted from Donald L. Staheli, "Obedience—Life's Great Challenge," *Ensign*, May 1998, 82.

8. "I'll Go Where You Want Me to Go," *Hymns*, no. 270.

Our purpose for which we were called and predestined may be aligned with our current path or a departure from it. For example, a doctor may feel moved to leave their practice and offer free medical care to indigent people. Or that same doctor may be moved to discontinue practicing medicine altogether to work in the Church's educational system. This calling is most often revealed to us by the Spirit during our journey inward, and unlike other callings, it is not normally extended to us by the bishopric or stake presidency.

As we pick through the rubble of our lives and gather what is most precious to us, we begin to see how our experiences have purified, shaped, and sharpened us. We see that the tests and trials in our life that we once thought stemmed from the neglect of an unconcerned God, or were inflicted by an unfair Father, were actually the Goldsmith's refining fires and the Gardener's tender pruning. We begin to see how His tender, ever-guiding hand in our lives has brought us to this moment, and we begin to sense who we are meant to be. We begin to hear the echoes from our premortal life when our Father asked, "Whom shall I send, and who will go for us?" And we, like the Savior, responded, "Here am I; send me" (Isaiah 6:8). At that time, some of us may have been among "the noble and great ones" (Abraham 3:22; Doctrine and Covenants 138:55) who committed to some grand purpose that affected everyone. Others of us may have committed to help a single person in a cause that was no less noble.

My Journey Inward

As I reflect on my life, I recognize that over twenty years ago, I felt the desire to write a leadership book and speak on a lecture circuit. I then changed my career and became a trainer so I could sharpen my speaking skills. I pursued my education, including a master's of science in organizational leadership, so I would have the knowledge and credentials to support the assertions I would write in my book. I changed companies six times seeking the opportunity to focus solely on leadership development instead of mingling leadership with technical training. And finally, just three years ago, I wrote my book—only to have it wrenched from my hands.

For some time, I felt God had abandoned me. I had served faithfully in all that He had required of me. I had responded to the whisperings of the Holy Ghost and followed the paths He had laid before me. I had done all He had asked of me, and all I wanted in return was to have my children be faithful members of the Church, to be respected in the Church and in my chosen profession, and to achieve my goal to write a best-selling leadership book. It seemed like all was going so well. I was on the cusp of achieving all of those things when everything fell apart. Why did He bring me so close to Self-Actualization only to cause my world to crash down around me?

During my journey inward, I began to understand "precept upon precept; line upon line . . . here a little, and there a little" (Isaiah 28:10) how God had prepared me for who He wanted me to be and who I had committed to be in the premortal life. He helped me see that each of my goals were what *I* wanted. It was "my will be done," not "Thy will be done." Because I was so selfish, it was necessary for Him to use my selfish desires to steer me in the direction He needed me to go.

As I began to emerge from my dark night, I was sharing what I was learning about the dark night with Elizabeth, my loving and ever-supportive wife, who was still in her dark night. She said to me, "I'm not sure how, but I think your experience with the dark night will affect what you do with the rest of your life." I then began to think differently. Maybe God did not intend for me to write a leadership book. Maybe He intended for me to write a book about the stages of faith and the dark night of the soul. But twenty years ago, I would not have understood if He had said to me, "I want you to write a book about the dark night of the soul." Instead, He put in me the desire to write a book. I chose leadership as the topic. He then called me to various leadership callings in the Church, not to gratify my pride and vain ambition (see Doctrine and Covenants 121:37) but to expose me to those who were in the depths of the dark night so I could see its effects. He then brought me near to Self-Actualization and then brought my world down around me to thrust me into the dark night so I could experience it for myself. He introduced me to mentors and authors to teach me about the dark night. Then He helped me write this book through the influence of the Spirit so that I might share what I had learned and so He could teach me what I had yet to learn.

My journey inward revealed that this is what the Lord wanted me to do—perhaps what I was foreordained to do in the premortal life. I have come to believe that, in the work of salvation, there are no co-incidences.[9] It is now evident to me that the events in my life over the last twenty years were divinely orchestrated and not just random life experiences. They purified me as much as I would permit them to and prepared me to write this book. This book may never be a bestseller, but if it helps just one person endure the dark night of the soul, then that is enough. For "the worth of souls is great in the sight of God" (Doctrine and Covenants 18:10), and I believe He may orchestrate the events in our lives over decades to prepare us to help just one of His children. When we stop looking back mournfully at the painful things in our life and look forward hopefully to who might benefit from our experiences, we begin to see the hand of God at work and

> *In the work of salvation, there are no coincidences.*

---

9. See David A. Bednar, "The Tender Mercies of the Lord," *Ensign* or *Liahona*, May 2005, 99.

become instruments in His hands to bring about His eternal purposes.

The hallmarks of the journey inward are healing and self-discovery. The wisdom we have gained over time helps us see the hand of God at work, and we recognize and accept who He wants us to be.

> *When we stop looking back mournfully at the painful things in our life and look forward hopefully to who might benefit from our experiences, we begin to see the hand of God at work and become instruments in His hands to bring about His eternal purposes.*

STAGNATION DURING THE JOURNEY INWARD

We can become stagnant during our journey inward, especially if we resist who He wants us to be. Consider the story of Jonah. The Lord wanted him to warn the people of Nineveh to repent (see Jonah 1:2). Jonah didn't want to go to Nineveh, so he fled "from the presence of the Lord" (verse 3) in a ship to Tarshish. Then there arose "a mighty tempest in the sea, so that the ship was like to be broken" (verse 4). When the ship's panicked crew learned that Jonah's God had caused the storm, they reluctantly cast Jonah overboard (see verses 7–15). Once they did, "the sea ceased from her raging" (verse 15) and Jonah was swallowed by a whale (see verse 17).

Jonah was in the belly of the whale for three days and nights. He described his experience in Jonah 2:3–5: "For thou hadst cast me into the deep, in the midst of the seas; and the floods compassed me about: all thy billows and thy waves passed over me. Then I said, I am cast out of thy sight. . . . The waters compassed me about, even to the soul: the depth closed me round about."

Jonah's dark night of the soul began in the belly of the whale. Note his helplessness as he was overcome by his circumstances, his feeling that God had abandoned him, and his descent in the dark depths—all common experiences in the dark night of the soul.

After the whale spat him out, Jonah obediently went to Nineveh and warned the people to repent or the city would be overthrown (see Jonah 3:3). The people repented and the Lord spared them (see Jonah 3:10), but Jonah was angry (see Jonah 4:3). Apparently, Jonah went where he was told to go and did what he was told to do, but he did not become who the Lord wanted him to be. Jonah was like an impetuous adolescent who, when told to clean his room, slams the bedroom door, shoves his dirty clothes under the bed, and scornfully throws his scattered shoes and sports equipment in his closet without ever appreciating the serenity of a clean room. Jonah wanted Nineveh to be destroyed and could not feel "joy in the soul that repenteth" (Doctrine and Covenants 18:13). They had been a wicked people and ruthless enemies of Israel who deserved God's vengeance. Also, Jonah had just prophesied that the city would be destroyed. Not destroying the city would call into question his prophecy and legitimacy as a prophet.

The Lord tried to reason with Jonah, but he would not yield. In his anger and despair, he cried out, "Therefore now, O Lord, take, I beseech thee, my life from me; for it is better for me to die than to live" (Jonah 4:3).

Jonah then "went out of the city" (Jonah 4:5) and picked a spot where he could see what would become of it. He constructed a booth, a shelter of branches and leaves, to provide some protection from the sun. Still suffering the effects of the dark night of the soul, he sat there sulking, hoping God would come to His senses and reap vengeance on Nineveh.

Despite Jonah's tantrum, the Lord was still kind and merciful to him. Overnight, He "prepared a gourd, and made it to come up over

Jonah, that it might be a shadow over his head, to deliver him from his grief" (Jonah 4:4'). This gourd was a shrub with broad leaves, a plant that "quickly springs up to the size of a small tree."[10] This kindness made Jonah "exceedingly glad" (verse 6).

The Lord, desiring to spur Jonah out of the dark night and into the journey inward, "prepared a worm when the morning rose the next day, and it smote the gourd that it withered" (verse 7). He then caused the sun to "beat upon the head of Jonah" (verse 8) and sent "a vehement east wind" (verse 8) to accelerate his dehydration. Jonah mourned the withered gourd and, in the heat of the day, "fainted, and wished in himself to die, and said, It is better for me to die than to live" (verse 8).

Jonah, now "compelled to be humble" (Alma 32:13), was ready to begin the journey inward and learn what the Lord was teaching him. The Lord asked Jonah, "Doest thou well to be angry for the gourd? And he said, I do well to be angry, even unto death. Then said the Lord, Thou hast had pity on the gourd, for the which thou hast not laboured, neither madest it grow; which came up in a night, and perished in a night: And should not I spare Nineveh, that great city, wherein are more than sixscore thousand persons?" (Jonah 4:9–11).

Jonah finally understood the Lord's lesson of love, compassion, and mercy. He could see how his selfishness obscured his perception of the Lord's great work "to bring to pass the immortality and eternal life of man" (Moses 1:39). He understood that he had supplanted "Thy will be done" with "my will be done." He now knew who the Lord wanted him to be, and he regretted that he did what the Lord wanted him to do without first becoming who he was meant to be.

Jonah, recalling the events surrounding his dark night, rejoiced: "When my soul fainted within me I remembered the Lord: and my

---

10. "Kikayon," Wikimedia Foundation, last modified May 18, 2022, https://en.wikipedia.org/wiki/Kikayon.

prayer came in unto thee, into thine holy temple. They that observe lying vanities forsake their own mercy. But I will sacrifice unto thee with the voice of thanksgiving; I will pay that that I have vowed. Salvation is of the Lord" (Jonah 2:7–9).

Like Jonah, we can become stagnant during our journey inward. We can experience discouragement, negativity, and self-absorption. We may experience increased doubt, but our doubts can also lead to greater faith.

THE JOURNEY OUTWARD

The second phase of the Adult stage of faith is the journey outward. Our journey inward *revealed* who the Lord wanted us to be; our journey outward is about *becoming* who He wants us to be. We still desire to achieve Self-Actualization, but our vision of what we would become transforms into who He wants us to become. Gradually and then suddenly, Self-Actualization is within our reach as we commit to His vision for us. As we shed our selfishness, supplant "my will be done" with "Thy will be done," and let go of our ego, we begin to step out of ourselves and back into the world with our newfound vision and purpose. We become all the Lord wants us to be and do all the Lord wants us to do.

> It may not be on the mountain height
> Or over the stormy sea,
> It may not be at the battle's front
> My Lord will have need of me.
> But if, by a still, small voice he calls
> To paths that I do not know,
> I'll answer, dear Lord, with my hand in thine:
> I'll go where you want me to go.[11]

---

11. "I'll Go Where You Want Me to Go," *Hymns*, no. 270.

The journey outward is the opposite of the Young Adult stage of faith. In the Young Adult stage, we do what the Lord wants us to do in order to be who *we* want to be. During our journey outward, our ego dissolves and we do what the Lord wants us to do in order to be who *He* wants us to be. Gradually, we again begin to serve with all our "heart, might, mind and strength" (Doctrine and Covenants 4:2) as we did in the Young Adult stage. However, perhaps for the first time, we serve "with an eye single to the glory of God" (Doctrine and Covenants 4:5). We are less motivated by our need for Esteem and "do not [our] alms before men, to be seen of them" (Matthew 6:1). We do not seek credit or recognition; instead, we do our service "in secret" (Matthew 6:3). We are content with the knowledge that our Father in Heaven is pleased with our service, and that is enough. We just quietly go where the Lord wants us to go and do what He wants us to do.

For this reason, I feel a twinge of discomfort when I speak of myself or share my personal experiences. After emerging from the dark night and finishing the inward journey, I find I am less apt to turn the spotlight on myself. I have always been the kind of person who enjoyed the spotlight, and there remains in me more selfishness than I would like to admit; but more of my self-serving nature has been purged from me than I thought possible. Learning to serve behind the scenes without credit or recognition has been a necessary but difficult part of the personal purification process in my spiritual journey.

During our outward journey, we are content to serve in secret, but our divine calling may put us in the public eye. Dr. Martin Luther King Jr. was a preacher who became a champion for civil rights. The day before his assassination, King gave a sermon titled "I've Been to the Mountaintop." In that speech, he expressed his hope to live a bit longer, an indirect acknowledgement that there were some plotting to take his life. He had been stabbed a decade before, and on the day of that speech, his plane was delayed because of a bomb threat. It was apparent to him that those who sought to take his life were closing in around him. In his sermon he said:

> Like anybody, I would like to live a long life. Longevity has its place. But I'm not concerned about that now. I just want to do God's will. And He's allowed me to go up to the mountain. And I've looked over. And I've seen the promised land. I may not get there with you. But I want you to know tonight, that we, as a people, will get to the promised land. So I'm happy, tonight. I'm not worried about anything. I'm not fearing any man. Mine eyes have seen the glory of the coming of the Lord.[12]

At another time he said, "Yes, Jesus, I want to be on your right or your left side, not for any selfish reason. I want to be on your right or your best side, not in terms of some political kingdom or ambition. But I just want to be there in love and in justice and in truth and in commitment to others, so that we can make of this old world a new world."[13]

Note that he only wanted to do the will of God and was unconcerned about himself. He also explained he had no selfish motives, but rather his motives were love for others, justice, and truth; his commitment to serve others; and his desire to make the world better. These are all hallmarks of the outward journey.

Dr. J. Kameron Carter, professor of theology and Black church studies at Duke Divinity School, explained, "King . . . wasn't trying to lead a black nationalist movement. For that matter, King wasn't trying to lead any political movement. He was a preacher—a churchman."[14] As with King, our outward journey may take us "to paths that [we]

---

12. Brandon Ambrosino, "How Martin Luther King Jr.'s faith drove his activism," Vox, Jan. 19, 2015, https://www.vox.com/2015/1/19/7852311/martin-luther-king-faith.

13. Ambrosino, "How Martin Luther King Jr.'s faith drove his activism."

14. Ambrosino, "How Martin Luther King Jr.'s faith drove his activism."

do not know."[15] We may be called to champion a cause, move to a new community, or change our profession. For example, a schoolteacher may leave the classroom to combat human trafficking. A CEO may leave their corporation to work with a community food bank. A stay-at-home parent who had planned to start their career when their youngest entered high school may feel moved to forego that opportunity to tutor a special needs child in their community. Our Father may have a plan for us that is quite different from the plan we had for ourselves. On our outward journey, we go where He wants us to go and do what He wants us to do in order to be who He wants us to be.

Consider the words of James: "Go to now, ye that say, To day or to morrow we will go into such a city, and continue there a year, and buy and sell, and get gain: Whereas ye know not what shall be on the morrow. For what is your life? It is even a vapour, that appeareth for a little time, and then vanisheth away. For that ye ought to say, If the Lord will, we shall live, and do this, or that" (James 4:13–15).

Increased Love

One of the most significant hallmarks of our journey outward is increased love for others. King Benjamin taught that as we "come to the knowledge of the glory of God" and "have known of his goodness and have tasted of his love" (Mosiah 4:11), we are "filled with the love of God" (Mosiah 4:12). We will then "succor those that stand in need of [our] succor; [we] will administer of [our] substance unto him that standeth in need; and [we] will not suffer that the beggar putteth up his petition to [us] in vain, and turn him out to perish" (Mosiah 4:16).

As we are filled with His love, we find we are more compassionate, more apt to serve, less judgmental, more appreciative of others' gifts, more patient, more trusting, and more forgiving. We begin to

---

15. "I'll Go Where You Want Me to Go," *Hymns*, no. 270.

see others through God's eyes and value their infinite worth. We sense our Father's desire to bless them and bring them safely home to Him. We feel our responsibility shift from saving them to helping them feel His infinite love, grace, and mercy so they themselves will yearn for salvation.

Our love compels us to serve others even when some say they should help themselves. We trust others even when some call us naive. We sacrifice for others even when some claim they take advantage of us. We give others the benefit of the doubt when some assume they intended the worst.

As a prerequisite to loving others, we also develop greater love for ourselves. Jesus taught the "first and great commandment" (Matthew 22:38) is to "love the Lord thy God with all thy heart, and with all thy soul, and with all thy mind" (verse 37) and the second commandment is to "love thy neighbour as thyself" (verse 39). Though not stated explicitly, the third commandment is to love thyself because we cannot love our neighbors as ourselves until we first love ourselves. Loving ourselves includes defining our individual worth, celebrating and improving our talents, accepting our flaws, forgiving ourselves, appreciating how beautiful we are regardless of how the world may momentarily define beauty, and liking ourselves even if some do not. In the dark night, it is difficult to love ourselves because we are consumed with self-pity, self-loathing, and self-doubt. As we begin to emerge from the dark night, we realize we felt those self-destructive emotions because we were self-serving and self-absorbed. It was all about us. Learning that it is not about us is the most liberating discovery that frees us from self-pity, self-loathing, and self-doubt.

> *Learning that it is not about us is the most liberating discovery that frees us from self-pity, self-loathing, and self-doubt.*

During our journey outward, we shift our focus from inside to outside. We then look for who we can help instead of who can help us. Ironically, as our love and concern for others increases, so also does our love for ourselves. We are less judgmental of ourselves, more appreciative of our gifts, more patient with ourselves, and more forgiving of ourselves. We begin to see ourselves through God's eyes and value our infinite worth. We acknowledge our sins and imperfections, but we are less discouraged by them and more encouraged by God's infinite love, mercy, grace, and the Atonement of Christ.

STAGNATION DURING OUR OUTWARD JOURNEY

We cannot become stagnant during our outward journey. We are serving outside of ourselves. We are doing the will of God. We have an others-first mindset that causes us to be less concerned about our own wants and desires. We are relatively unfazed by trials of life that would have incapacitated us in earlier years. We are part of something infinitely larger and eternal that makes this life's minor challenges seem insignificant. It is a liberating stage that frees us from the bonds of our egos, our selfish desires, and our ever-increasing measures of worldly success.

> *The Adult stage of faith is a liberating stage that frees us from the bonds of our egos, our selfish desires, and our ever-increasing measures of worldly success.*

CRISIS AT THE ADULT STAGE

We would suppose that the blissful Adult stage would not lead to a crisis of faith; but as with all of the previous stages, we experience a crisis as we begin to transition to the next and final stage. As we embark on our outward journey, others initially appreciate our renewed relationship with God, respect our evolution from self-serving to serving, and admire our commitment to help others. Our ward leaders appreciate our quiet service behind the scenes and value our wisdom. We quietly continue our work following the whisperings of the Spirit. We seek only God's approval and no longer "aspire to the honors of men" (Doctrine and Covenants 121:35).

COUNTER-CULTURE

As our walk with God becomes more in sync with His will, we become more out of sync with the Pharisaic traditions (see Mark 7:3) in the Church. We become counter-culture. We become less interested in the latest stake or ward programs, we are unconcerned with cultural norms, we are unfazed by minor issues others choke on (see Matthew 23:24), and we are disinterested in debates over doctrine, policy, and procedure. We trivialize the issues others believe are urgent and important because we see they have little impact on eternal life.

We no longer feel the need to "practice" religion. The disciplines that served us well in the earlier stages of faith evolve from rituals to natural communion with God. For example, we no longer think in terms of praying morning and night or studying our scriptures thirty minutes each day. Instead, we enjoy ongoing communication with God that may include formal prayer or informal conversation with Him throughout the day. As Amulek taught, "Let your hearts be full, drawn out in prayer unto him continually" (Alma 34:27). It is similar to working on a project with our supervisor in the same room. We are all working on our individual tasks to achieve the end goal, but periodically the supervisor gives us direction or an additional task, or we may ask a question or seek advice or make a suggestion. The conversation is not continuous, but the supervisor's guidance is. Similarly, we study the scriptures not because it is a daily ritual but to commune with God. Elder Robert D. Hales said, "When we want to speak to

God, we pray. And when we want Him to speak to us, we search the scriptures."[16] We speak to God through prayer. He speaks to us through the scriptures.

During our outward journey, we are more peaceful and patient. To others, it may seem we are out of touch with reality because we do not get caught up in the whirlwind of the current issues. We have an eternal perspective. We acknowledge that we have "seen all the works that are done under the sun; and, behold, all is vanity and vexation of spirit" (Ecclesiastes 1:14).

Ironically, as we become firmer in the faith and draw nearer to God, our counter-culture behaviors may lead others to believe our faith is failing and we are distancing ourselves from Him. Those in the Young Adult stage of faith equate spirituality to activity, specifically action and involvement in the Church. They demonstrate their faith by their works (see James 2:18). Therefore, they assume our faith is lacking because they cannot see our faith in our works. They do not see our work behind the scenes, and we may not participate in the latest program or promote the latest policy. To them, it appears as though we are less active and have drifted off the straight and narrow path, though in reality it is quite the opposite.

Jesus was the only perfect person to walk the earth. Though He was the King of Kings and Lord of Lords (see Revelation 16:19), He came to serve, not to be served (see Mark 10:44–45). Despite his perfection, infinite love, selfless service, and His giving the ultimate sacrifice in our behalf, He was accused of being gluttonous (see Matthew 11:19), a drunkard (see Matthew 11:19), a liar (see John 8:13), a false prophet (see Luke 7:36–39), possessed (see Mark 3:22), blasphemous (see Matthew 23:63–66), of violating the Sabbath (see Matthew

16. Robert D. Hales, "Holy Scriptures: The Power of God unto Our Salvation," *Ensign* or *Liahona*, Nov. 2006, 26.

12:1–14), associating with the wicked (see Luke 7:39), and wielding the power of Satan (see Matthew 12:22–28). Isaiah said of Him:

> He is despised and rejected of men; a man of sorrows, and acquainted with grief: and we hid as it were our faces from him; he was despised, and we esteemed him not.
>
> Surely he hath borne our griefs, and carried our sorrows: yet we did esteem him stricken, smitten of God, and afflicted.
>
> But he was wounded for our transgressions, he was bruised for our iniquities: the chastisement of our peace was upon him; and with his stripes we are healed.
>
> All we like sheep have gone astray; we have turned every one to his own way; and the Lord hath laid on him the iniquity of us all.
>
> He was oppressed, and he was afflicted, yet he opened not his mouth: he is brought as a lamb to the slaughter, and as a sheep before her shearers is dumb, so he openeth not his mouth.
>
> He was taken from prison and from judgment: and who shall declare his generation? for he was cut off out of the land of the living: for the transgression of my people was he stricken.
>
> And he made his grave with the wicked, and with the rich in his death; because he had done no violence, neither was any deceit in his mouth. (Isaiah 53:3–9)

We will never be as perfect, loving, selfless, and serving as Jesus was. We will never be as despised or rejected as He was or experience the depth of His sorrow and grief. But in the Adult stage of faith, the crisis we experience gives us a taste of His suffering. As we strive to be more like Him—more obedient, loving, selfless, and serving—we may feel less valued in the Church and less needed by those we love and want to serve. Our counter-culture beliefs and behaviors may put us out of step with the congregation and grate against those in leadership positions who are in the Adolescent and Young Adult stages of faith. They may begin to wonder if we have lost our way and may admonish us to get in line and be "anxiously engaged" (Doctrine and Covenants 58:27).

Needs

In the Adult stage, we are content with God's approval, yet there remains in us a desire to fill our Social and Esteem needs. Our Social need is threatened when we find we are out of resonance with the congregation and no longer fit in as we did before. Our Esteem need is threatened as we want to give more and are less often called upon, or when we share our wisdom and knowledge and others think it is foolishness. We have so much to offer, yet they believe we have "turned out of the way" (Job 31:7) and "gone astray" (Isaiah 53:6).

This crisis is not as incapacitating as the dark night because our faith is firmer and our testimony fortifies us. We experience doubt in this crisis, as we do in each crisis of faith; however, in this crisis we doubt ourselves, not the gospel. We question our self-worth and our ability to continue to serve as we feel somewhat "despised and rejected of men" (Isaiah 53:3). In this crisis, like the Savior, we are downtrodden with "sorrows, and acquainted with grief" (Isaiah 53:3).

Regression

We find ourselves again at the crossroads: "go back," "go out," or "go forward." This time, "go out" is not an option. Our testimony is too firm to consider leaving the Church. "Go forward" is the best option, but the path forward is, as it was before, obscured by the fog of doubt and uncertainty. "Go back" is the most enticing alternative. Therefore, many of us return to an earlier stage of faith so we fit in a little better. We justify this regression, believing we can offer so much more than we did before because we are now equipped with the wisdom, knowledge, and experience we gained in the dark night.

As we regress to an earlier stage, we again find our place in the Church, which satisfies our Social need, and we may be afforded opportunities to use our talents in various assignments and callings, which satisfies our Esteem need. However, the plan of salvation is a plan of eternal *progression*, not *regression*. Our Father brought us to this point to go forward! Though it feels good to again fit in and be valued, we will sense something is amiss.

Consider the story of Mary and Martha. They invited Jesus to their home for dinner. Prior to dinner, Martha was busy in the kitchen "cumbered about much serving" (Luke 10:40) while Mary "sat as Jesus' feet, and heard His word" (Luke 10:39). Eventually, Martha became irritated with Mary and said to Jesus, "Lord, dost thou not care that my sister hath left me to serve alone? Bid her therefore that she help me. And Jesus answered and said unto her, Martha, Martha, thou art careful and troubled about many things: But one thing is needful: and Mary hath chosen that good part, which shall not be taken away from her" (Luke 10:40–42).

Martha was "anxiously engaged in a good cause" (Doctrine and Covenants 58:27), and her work was needful and noble. When we regress to an earlier stage of faith to escape the crisis at the Adult stage, like Martha we may find ourselves "cumbered about much serving" (Luke 10:40). As we are "anxiously engaged" in the needful and noble work, we will sense the Savior waiting for us to come and receive "that good part" (Luke 10:42).

ENDURING THE CRISIS

Enduring the crisis of faith in the Adult stage requires us to reframe Self-Actualization. In the Adult stage, we shift our mindset from "my will be done" to "Thy will be done." We respond to our Father's calling, and we go where He wants us to go, do what He wants us to do, and become who He wants us to become. We reframe Self-Actualization by aligning our vision of ourself with God's vision of us. In essence, His calling becomes our dream. That means we may need to shed whatever we once wanted to be and replace that goal with the work God has called us to. When we do, our Social and Esteem needs no longer feel threatened when we do not quite fit into the Church, when others disregard our knowledge or wisdom, or when we are not considered for assignments or opportunities. We know we have chosen "that good part," and we are closer to Self-Actualization than we have ever been.

KEY POINT SUMMARY

- In the Adult stage of faith, we apply the wisdom we have gained throughout our lifetime.
- We discover our divine purpose and respond to our divine call.
- Selfishness decreases and our love for others increases.
- We may become counter-culture and be tempted to regress.

8

THE SENIOR STAGE OF FAITH

"If we empty our hearts of self, God will fill them with His love."

—Charles Spurgeon[1]

"The whole being of any Christian is faith and love. Faith brings the person to God, love brings the person to people."

—Martin Luther[2]

In human development, the elder stage of life is when we have lived past the ambitions of our youth and settled comfortably into our remaining years. Perhaps we are retired and free from climbing the corporate ladder, playing office politics, and dealing with the ever-present pressure of performance and profits.

Though we may have some regrets, we are quite content. We enjoy life and time with family and friends. The bruises and scars we

---

1. Charles Spurgeon, "If we empty," AZ Quotes, accessed Nov. 9, 2022, https://www.azquotes.com/quote/703872.

2. "35 Martin Luther Quotes On Prayer, Reformation, Marriage, Faith," Overall Motivation, accessed Nov. 10, 2022, https://www.overallmotivation.com/quotes/martin-luther-quotes-prayer-reformation-marriage-faith/.

received in the battles of life are fading. What remains is the invaluable wisdom we have gained through those experiences. We are apt to serve and have much to offer. We are full of love, patience, and compassion.

The Senior stage of faith is epitomized by the image of a loving grandmother. I think of a dear sister, Marge Means, who was in my ward. She had snow-white hair, a sweet voice, and a kind, persistent smile. She and her husband were serving in the addiction recovery program and were responsible for facilitating regular meetings and supporting those who were in recovery. We were once discussing their calling. She described some of the things they were doing in the program and then said, "What they deal with is so difficult. I'm only grateful I was blessed with different challenges." Her tone conveyed deep compassion and love for them without any hint of judgment or impatience. I thought to myself, *I hope I will someday love others as deeply as she does.*

At her funeral some years later, one of the speakers shared a story about her. He said that after her passing, the men who collected her garbage stopped by her home to express their condolences. They explained they called her *abuela*, grandmother in Spanish. Apparently, each week when they would come to collect the trash, she would bring them sandwiches and drinks. No one besides these men knew of this little act of kindness. It left us to wonder what other acts of love and kindness this dear sister was performing behind the scenes.

COMPASSION AND UNCONDITIONAL LOVE

Compassion and unconditional love are the hallmarks of the Senior stage of faith. Stephen R. Robinson noted:

The Prime Directive has been delivered to us pointedly by the Savior no fewer than three times in John's Gospel alone: "A new commandment I give unto you, That ye love one another; as I have loved you, that ye also love one another. By this shall all men know that ye are my disciples, if ye have love one to another" (John 13:34-35). "This is my commandment, That ye love one another, as I have loved you. Greater love hath no man than this, that a man lay down his life for his friends" (John 15:12-13). "These things I command you, that ye love one another" (John 15:17). . . .

This is not emotional fluff. This is not pie in the sky, wishful thinking, or idealistic gas. Love is not some subsidiary principle that allows the weepy among us to go off on a crying jag. It's not just something thrown in for the benefit of the sisters or for the super-sensitive "artsy" types. It is not an option that may be ignored by those who would prefer not to clutter their lives with other peoples' problems. There is a grand key here, probably the grandest of them all. It is this: the heart and soul of the gospel is love, and all the rest is commentary. Whatever else we may perceive religion to be, we are wrong—for true religion is love in action—God's love for us and our love for God and for our neighbors."[3]

Christ's gospel is the gospel of love. John taught:

Beloved, let us love one another: for love is of God; and every one that loveth is born of God, and knoweth God.

He that loveth not knoweth not God; for God is love.

In this was manifested the love of God toward us, because that God sent his only begotten Son into the world, that we might live through him.

Herein is love, not that we loved God, but that he loved us, and sent his Son to be the propitiation for our sins.

Beloved, if God so loved us, we ought also to love one another. (1 John 4:7–11)

The Lord taught that the greatest commandments are to love God and to love our neighbor as we love ourselves (see Matthew 22:36–40). He explained that "on these two commandments hang all the

---

3. Stephen E. Robinson, *Following Christ: The Parable of the Divers and More Good News* (Salt Lake City: Deseret Book, 2004), 137–138.

law and the prophets" (Matthew 22:40). In other words, every law of God is simply a reminder of how to show love for Him, others, and ourselves. Paul explained:

> Love one another: for he that loveth another hath fulfilled the law.
>
> For this, Thou shalt not commit adultery, Thou shalt not kill, Thou shalt not steal, Thou shalt not bear false witness, Thou shalt not covet; and if there be any other commandment, it is briefly comprehended in this saying, namely, Thou shalt love thy neighbour as thyself.
>
> Love worketh no ill to his neighbour: therefore love is the fulfilling of the law. (Romans 13:8–10)

In truth, there is only one commandment: *thou shalt love.* If we could simply learn to truly love God, others, and ourselves, there would be no need for other carnal commandments.

CHARITY, THE PURE LOVE OF CHRIST

In the Senior stage of faith, we have "a perfect brightness of hope, and a love of God and of all men" (2 Nephi 31:20). This unconditional love is charity, "the pure love of Christ" (Moroni 7:47). Paul said that of faith, hope, and charity, "the greatest of these is charity" (1 Corinthians 13:13). As noted earlier, hope leads to faith. In fact, Mormon explained we cannot have faith unless we first have hope (see Moroni 7:40). If hope leads to faith, then perhaps Paul was implying that faith leads to charity. If so, each of the stages of faith and their associated crises are designed to help us develop charity—selfless, sacrificial, unconditional love.

> *In truth, there is only one commandment: thou shalt love. If we could simply learn to truly love God, others, and ourselves, there would be no need for other carnal commandments.*

Enos's experience most succinctly demonstrates one's evolution from hope to charity, from self-serving to serving, and from conditional love to unconditional love. Enos's father, Jacob, gave Enos the Nephite record, the first part of which would become the Book of Mormon. Enos promised his father he would maintain and add to the record, but apparently, at some point, Enos experienced a crisis of faith, and at the crossroads, he chose to "go out" of the Church instead of "go back" or "go forward." Though Enos's record does not explicitly state he apostatized, most assume that he did. President Spencer W. Kimball said of him, "Like many sons of good families he strayed. How heinous were his sins I do not know, but they must have been grievous."[4]

> *Each of the stages of faith and their associated crises are designed to help us develop charity—selfless, sacrificial, unconditional love.*

After some time passed, Enos was hunting, and "the words which [he] had often heard [his] father speak concerning eternal life, and the joy of the saints, sunk deep into [his] heart" (Enos 1:3). This gave him hope, and his "soul hungered" (verse 4) for redemption. His hope fed his faith, and he kneeled down and cried unto God for the welfare of his "own soul" (verse 4). He prayed all day and into the night until he finally heard the voice of God declare, "Enos, thy sins are forgiven thee, and thou shalt be blessed" (verse 5).

After he received forgiveness, he began to plead in behalf of his family and friends, those he loved and those who loved him (see verse 9). Once he obtained a blessing for them, his "faith began to be unshaken in the Lord" (verse 11). He then began to pray with equal fervency for his enemies, the Lamanites, whose "hatred was fixed" (verse 20) upon his people and who continually sought to destroy them. He

---

4. Spencer W. Kimball, "Prayer," *New Era*, Mar. 1978.

described them as ferocious, bloodthirsty, and filthy (see verse 20). Despite this, he prayed fervently for their welfare until God promised He would preserve the Nephite records and "bring them forth [to redeem] the Lamanites in his own due time" (verse 16).

After his prayer, Enos was "wrought upon by the power of God [to] preach and prophesy unto [the] people, and declare the word according to the truth which is in Christ. And [he] declared it in all [his] days, and . . . rejoiced in it above that of the world" (Enos 1:26).

Notice how Enos spiritually evolved from doubt, to hope, to belief, to unshakable faith, to selfless and lifelong service to God. Simultaneously, he evolved from loving himself, to loving those close to him, to loving his enemies. Enos's autobiography succinctly outlines everyone's spiritual journey. Our Father would have each of us evolve as Enos did. He wants us to move from doubt to unshakable faith, from self-serving to selfless service, and from loving ourselves to loving our enemies. Consider the parable of the Good Samaritan:

> And, behold, a certain lawyer stood up, and tempted [Jesus], saying, Master, what shall I do to inherit eternal life?
>
> He said unto him, What is written in the law? how readest thou?
>
> And he answering said, Thou shalt love the Lord thy God with all thy heart, and with all thy soul, and with all thy strength, and with all thy mind; and thy neighbour as thyself.
>
> And he said unto him, Thou hast answered right: this do, and thou shalt live.
>
> But he, willing to justify himself, said unto Jesus, And who is my neighbour?
>
> And Jesus answering said, A certain man went down from Jerusalem to Jericho, and fell among thieves, which stripped him of his raiment, and wounded him, and departed, leaving him half dead.
>
> And by chance there came down a certain priest that way: and when he saw him, he passed by on the other side.

And likewise a Levite, when he was at the place, came and
looked on him, and passed by on the other side.

But a certain Samaritan, as he journeyed, came where he was:
and when he saw him, he had compassion on him,

And went to him, and bound up his wounds, pouring in oil
and wine, and set him on his own beast, and brought him to an
inn, and took care of him.

And on the morrow when he departed, he took out two pence,
and gave them to the host, and said unto him, Take care of him;
and whatsoever thou spendest more, when I come again, I will
repay thee.

Which now of these three, thinkest thou, was neighbour unto
him that fell among the thieves?

And he said, He that shewed mercy on him. Then said Jesus
unto him, Go, and do thou likewise. (Luke 10:25–37)

A cursory reading of this parable might lead one to believe that the
point is to love thy neighbor. But the point of the parable is not love
thy *neighbor*; it is love thy *enemy*. The Jews and Samaritans despised
each other. In fact, it was unlawful for Jews to keep company with
Gentiles (see Acts 10:28), and Samaritans were considered even worse
than Gentiles because they were of mixed race—half-Jew and half-
Gentile. Therefore, "the Jews [had] no dealings with the Samaritans"
(John 4:9), and they gave one another good reason. Josephus, a Jewish
historian born about the time of Jesus's crucifixion, reported a number
of unpleasant events that fueled their reciprocal hatred. Samaritans
harassed Jewish pilgrims traveling through Samaria between Galilee
and Judea. They scattered human bones in the Jerusalem sanctuary,
which was the highest degree of defilement for the Jews.[5] Jews in turn
burned down Samaritan villages.[6] They would not allow Samaritans

5. See "Corpse uncleanness," Wikimedia Foundation, last modified July 21,
   2022, https://en.wikipedia.org/wiki/Corpse_uncleanness.

6. See Jürgen K. Zangenberg, "The Samaritans," Bible Odyssey, accessed Nov.
   9, 2022, https://www.bibleodyssey.org/en/people/related-articles/samaritans.

to be witnesses in the Jewish courts, they publicly cursed Samaritans in their synagogues, and they would not proselytize to them, which, as far as the Jews believed, excluded the Samaritans from the hope of eternal life. The phrase "thou art a Samaritan and hast a devil" was the Jews' default insult when they were unable to articulate a more specific reproach,[7] an insult the Pharisees spat at Jesus (see John 8:48).

Jesus's choice to make the Samaritan the hero in this parable was purposefully incendiary. In doing so, he simultaneously chastised the lawyer's self-righteousness and the Jews' deeply entrenched racism. Jesus trapped the lawyer with His question: "Which now of these three, thinkest thou, was neighbour unto him that fell among the thieves?" (Luke 10:36).

Though the answer was obvious, the lawyer could not answer the question directly for several reasons. First, the answer would undermine the appearance of righteousness that he worked so hard to maintain. Everyone present knew that the lawyer did not love his neighbor to the degree Jesus specified in the parable and therefore was in violation of the law as He defined it. Second, this lawyer was an expert in the law of Moses and was likely a Pharisee who believed that the oral traditions were equal to the written law. To say the Samaritan was the neighbor would undermine his conviction to the oral law, which included the tradition that it was unlawful for Jews to keep company with Gentiles (see Acts 10:28). Third, the lawyer could not avoid answering by stating he did not know, as they had done at other times (see Mark 11:27–33). He was likely one of the most learned men in the community, and to appear ignorant when the answer was so obvious would undermine his intellectual authority. Unable to say "the Samaritan," which was the obvious answer, the lawyer evasively stated, "He that shewed mercy on him" (Luke 10:37).

---

7. John McClintock and James Strong, *Cyclopedia of Biblical, Theological, and Ecclesiastical Literature*, vol. IX (New York: Harper and Brothers, 1880), 286.

In this parable, Jesus taught the lawyer to have charity, the "pure love of Christ" (Moroni 7:47). To have charity is to love everyone unconditionally. Therefore, to have charity is more than loving thy neighbor as thyself; it is loving thy *enemy* as thyself. Jesus taught, "Ye have heard that it hath been said, Thou shalt love thy neighbour, and hate thine enemy. But I say unto you, Love your enemies, bless them that curse you, do good to them that hate you, and pray for them which despitefully use you, and persecute you" (Matthew 5:43–44).

In the Senior stage of faith, we have charity. We love our enemies as ourselves and "frankly forgive" (1 Nephi 7:21) all who hurt or offend us. As the Roman soldiers lifted Jesus upon the cross, He cried out, "Father, forgive them; for they know not what they do" (Luke 23:34). In the same way, we "will not have a mind to injure one another, but to live peaceably" (Mosiah 4:13) because we are "filled with the love of God" (Mosiah 4:12). Therefore, we will "pray for them which despitefully use [us], and persecute [us]" (Matthew 5:44), for "charity suffereth long, and is kind . . . is not easily provoked, thinketh no evil . . . beareth all things, [and] endureth all things" (Moroni 7:45).

King Benjamin explained that as we are filled with this love (see Mosiah 4:12), we will naturally care for those in need: "And also, ye yourselves will succor those that stand in need of your succor; ye will administer of your substance unto him that standeth in need; and ye will not suffer that the beggar putteth up his petition to you in vain, and turn him out to perish" (Mosiah 4:16)

Mormon, in his lecture on faith, hope, and charity, exhorted us to develop charity: "Behold I say unto you that he cannot have faith and hope, save he shall be meek, and lowly of heart. If so, his faith and hope is vain, for none is acceptable before God, save the meek and lowly in heart; and if a man be meek and lowly in heart, and confesses by the power of the Holy Ghost that Jesus is the Christ, he must needs have charity; for if he have not charity he is nothing; wherefore he must needs have charity" (Moroni 7:43–44).

Love, specifically charity, is both a commandment and an aspiration. Like the Lord's command to be perfect (see Matthew 5:48), Mormon's command to "have charity" (Moroni 7:44) is an instruction to develop this preeminent Christlike attribute. He adds, "Pray unto the Father with all the energy of heart, that ye may be filled with this love, which he hath bestowed upon all who are true followers of his Son, Jesus Christ" (Moroni 7:48).

Note that we must pray for charity and that God bestows it upon us. It is not an attribute we are born with. It is not just an emotion we may feel in various circumstances or for certain people. It is not just being kind, or compassionate, or sacrificing to help others, though those behaviors may be evidence of it. For most of us, it is an attribute that we are to intentionally develop over time as we shed our selfishness, align ourselves with His purposes, serve with an eye single to His glory, develop empathy through trials and tribulations, forgive those who may not deserve our forgiveness, and become all He intends for us to be. As we do, our "bowels [will] also be full of charity towards all men, and to the household of faith" (Doctrine and Covenants 121:45). We will be "filled with this love" (Moroni 7:48) and unable to bear the thought "that any human soul should perish" (Mosiah 28:3).

Therefore, in the Senior stage of faith, we "waste and wear out our lives" (Doctrine and Covenants 123:13) serving God and others. We are motivated by our unconditional love and know that when we "are in the service of [our] fellow beings [we] are only in the service of [our] God" (Mosiah 2:17).

Because we are filled with the pure love of Christ, we are discontent with shallow relationships. Instead, we seek to build deep, intimate relationships as we become involved in the lives of those around us. Our deep love for others lifts and encourages them.

BEATITUDES IN THE SENIOR STAGE

The Savior's Sermon on the Mount in Matthew 5–7 perfectly describes us in the Senior stage of faith. We are humble, meek, merciful, pure in heart, peacemakers, persecuted for righteousness' sake, the salt of the earth, and a light to the world. We hunger and thirst after righteousness. We forgive. When slapped in the face, we offer the other cheek. When someone takes from us, we give them more. We serve in secret. When we pray, we converse with God instead of offering vain repetitions. We care little for treasures on earth but lay up for ourselves treasures in heaven. We serve one Master and lose ourselves in His service. We seek first to build His kingdom and trust that all we need will be added to us. We worry about today and not about tomorrow, trusting tomorrow will take care of itself. We judge not. We bring forth good fruit. We do the will of the Father.

SELFLESSNESS

In the Senior stage, we no longer care for the things of the world. We are unconcerned about fame and fortune and feel little need to set and achieve goals. We are willing to consecrate all the Lord has blessed us with for the building up of the kingdom of God on earth and the establishment of Zion.

Consider the story of the widow's mite: "And [Jesus] looked up, and saw the rich men casting their gifts into the treasury. And he saw also a certain poor widow casting in thither two mites. And he said, Of a truth I say unto you, that this poor widow hath cast in more than they all: For all these have of their abundance cast in unto the offerings of God: but she of her penury hath cast in all the living that she had" (Luke 21:1–4).

In the Senior stage, we are willing to "cast in all the living that [we have]." We give everything without feeling it is a sacrifice. We give

God all because all is God's. All we want is His presence in our lives, to do His will, and to invite everyone to "come unto Christ" (Moroni 10:32). That is enough.

SPIRITUALITY

We enjoy the continuous conversation with God that we initiated in the Adult stage of faith. The Spirit is ever present in our lives. We become so accustomed to the Spirit's influence that we almost become oblivious to His presence. It is somewhat like being in a room that is warmer than it should be, but not uncomfortably so. We become accustomed to it and think nothing of it until someone else walks in the room and declares, "It's really warm in here." Then we respond, "Oh, I didn't notice." In the same way, we can become accustomed to the continuous presence of the Holy Ghost. We may not always notice His presence, but we certainly notice when He is not present!

TRANSCENDENCE

Throughout this book, we have connected each stage of faith to a need in Abraham Maslow's hierarchy of needs. In Maslow's later years, he added an additional level above Self-Actualization that he called Transcendence. Transcendence is the highest level of development on Maslow's hierarchy. It is serving instead of self-serving and is focused on a greater good. Maslow explained, "Transcendence refers to the very highest and most inclusive or holistic levels of human consciousness, behaving and relating, as ends rather than means, to oneself, to significant others, to human beings in general, to other species, to nature, and to the cosmos."[8]

---

8. Courtney E. Ackerman, "What is Self-Transcendence? Definition and 6 Examples," Positive Psychology, June 4, 2018, https://positivepsychology.com/self-transcendence/.

The Senior stage of faith is spiritual Transcendence. It is transcending all the self-serving motives at the lower levels of Maslow's hierarchy of needs: Physiological, Safety, Social, Esteem, and Self-Actualization. Operating at the Transcendence level enables us to give all without expecting anything in return.

FITTING IN

It would seem that everyone would love those in the Senior stage because they love so fully and serve so selflessly. However, it is quite the opposite. Unconditional love unhinges the world. In our society, we separate friend from foe. We marshal our friends to stand against our foes and protect us from them. Therefore, our friends cannot be friends of our foes, though it does happen from time to time. For example, when a married couple divorces, the couple may expect their mutual friends to choose a side, and some find themselves caught in the middle. Though they may not want to choose a side, their neutrality can cause contention with both parties. This is human nature. We are herd animals; we support and protect each other by congregating in a herd: a family, a church, a sports team, a combat unit, or a political party. A threat to one is a threat to all, and disloyalty is grounds for excommunication.

When we are in the Senior stage of faith, we love everyone and will not choose sides. Therefore, our friends may develop animosity for us because we love their enemies as much as we love them. Jesus loved everyone. He said to his disciples, "Love one another, as I have loved you. Greater love hath no man than this, that a man lay down his life for his friends" (John 15:13). He gave his life to save his friends *and* his enemies. There is no greater love than that.

Initially, the Pharisees respected Jesus. They called him Master and Rabbi (see Luke 19:39, John 3:2), a term of respect only ascribed to teachers among the Pharisees. Note how Nicodemus, a Pharisee and "a ruler of the Jews" (John 3:1) addressed Him: "Rabbi, we know that thou art a teacher come from God: for no man can do these miracles that thou doest, except God be with him" (John 3:2).

But the more Jesus demonstrated His unconditional love, the more the Pharisees despised him. Matthew, one of Jesus's twelve disciples and a publican, invited Jesus to his house for a great feast. He also invited other publicans. Publicans were tax collectors for Rome. The Jews despised publicans and excommunicated any Jew who became one (see Bible Dictionary, "Publicans"). The scribes and Pharisees were appalled when they saw Jesus and His disciples sitting and eating with the publicans. They asked, "Why do ye eat and drink with publicans and sinners? And Jesus answering said unto them, They that are whole need not a physician; but they that are sick. I came not to call the righteous, but sinners to repentance" (Luke 5:30–32).

The Pharisees and Sadducees, the leaders of the church and Jewish community, had become so self-righteous they could no longer tolerate the presence of those they considered sinful. This rendered them incapable of performing the very work they were called to do. They were like doctors who could not bear to be with sick people.

Jesus, though He was full of love, was intolerant of those who "outwardly [appeared] righteous unto men, but within [were] full of hypocrisy and iniquity" (Matthew 23:28). For this reason, the only church Jesus criticized during his mortal ministry was His own, and the only people he openly criticized were His church's leaders. Jesus described them as lazy hypocrites who only sought the praise of others. He said to the multitude and His disciples:

The scribes and the Pharisees sit in Moses' seat:
    All therefore whatsoever they bid you observe, that observe and do; but do not ye after their works: for they say, and do not.

> For they bind heavy burdens and grievous to be borne, and lay them on men's shoulders; but they themselves will not move them with one of their fingers.
>
> But all their works they do for to be seen of men: they make broad their phylacteries, and enlarge the borders of their garments,
>
> And love the uppermost rooms at feasts, and the chief seats in the synagogues,
>
> And greetings in the markets, and to be called of men, Rabbi, Rabbi. (Matthew 23:2–7)

Phylacteries were leather boxes that were strapped to the left arm and forehead during prayer (see Deuteronomy 11:18). Each contained four scriptural passages from the law of Moses—Exodus 13:1–10, 11–16 and Deuteronomy 6:4–9; 11:13-21—and reminded Israel "to bind the law to their heart and mind."[9] The "borders of their garments" (Numbers 15:38–39) referred to the "blue tassels tied to the four corners of their garments and were meant to be a constant reminder of God's commandments."[10] They apparently enlarged their phylacteries and tassels to impress others with their piousness.

In Matthew 23, Jesus criticized the scribes and Pharisees for claiming they were worthy of heaven when they were not, and for declaring unworthy those who were worthy of that reward (see verse 13). He condemned them for their strenuous efforts to convert others to the gospel only to make them as wicked as they (see verse 15). He called them "blind guides" (verse 16) and "fools" (verse 17). He accused them of choosing which oaths and covenants they believed were binding and disregarding the others and the sacredness of the temple (see verses 16–17). He chastised them for living only the letter of the law while omitting "the weightier matters" (verse 23) of mercy and faith. He called them "hypocrites" (verse 25) for appearing clean on

---

9. "Phylacteries and Tassels," Redeemer of Israel, Apr. 11, 2017, http://www. redeemerofisrael.org/2015/02/phylacteries-and-tassels.html.

10. "Phylacteries and Tassels."

the outside when they were full of corruption inside. And He declared that even though they built monuments to the prophets, they would have slain them in their day just as their fathers did (verses 29–32).

Jesus's lambasting of the scribes and Pharisees was motivated by his unconditional love for them and the people they were called to serve. His only desire was for them to repent that they might be worthy of the blessings of eternal life and, in turn, help others obtain the same reward. He reproved them "betimes with sharpness" (Doctrine and Covenants 121:43), and if they had repented and not slain Him, He would have afterward shown "an increase of love" (Doctrine and Covenants 121:43) for them.

Today, our ward and stake leaders are not like the scribes and Pharisees. It's true that they are not perfect, but most are humble and kind and strive to be Christlike. Many are in the earlier stages of faith, likely the Adolescent or Young Adult stage. This is as it should be since most of the members of the Church are also in the earlier stages of faith and relate best to leaders in similar stages.

Though our local leaders are not generally Pharisaic, some may reject those in the Senior stage of faith who demonstrate unconditional love, just as the Pharisees rejected Jesus. For example, as mentioned earlier, in 2015 the Church declared that those who entered same-sex marriages were apostates and subject to disciplinary action, and their children were not permitted to be blessed as infants or baptized until they were eighteen years old, and then only after receiving permission from the First Presidency.[11] One in the Senior stage of faith would have felt overwhelming love for those in the Church who struggled with same-sex attraction, their family and friends, and the children who were denied baptism. That person may gently express

11. Jennifer Dobner, "New Mormon policy makes apostates of married same-sex couples, bars children from rites," *The Salt Lake Tribune*, Nov. 6, 2015, https://archive.sltrib.com/article.php?id=3144035&itype=CMSID.

their disagreement with this policy publicly. One in the Senior stage may insist that we should love and accept everyone regardless of their sexual preference or marital status and that their children should have the opportunity to be blessed and baptized.

A bishop with Pharisaic tendencies could categorize that member's opposition as apostasy, "acting in clear and deliberate public opposition to the Church, its doctrine, its policies, or its leaders."[12] The bishop may counsel the member to align with the Church's policies, instruct the member not to speak in opposition to the Church's policies, or marginalize the member by excluding them from certain assignments and callings. The bishop, after receiving approval from the stake president, could hold a membership council to consider that member's standing in the Church. If the member's behavior was public, overt, belligerent, and repeated, the member could be excommunicated for apostasy.

The bishop may be acting with the best intentions and would be aligned with the Church's policies and practices. If he is in the Child, Adolescent, or Young Adult stage of faith, obedience is the preeminent Christlike attribute, and to not uphold the law or hold others to it would compromise his integrity and his demonstration of faith.

Four years after that initial announcement regarding same-sex attraction, the Church announced changes to the policy.[13] The new policy stated that children of parents who identify as lesbian, gay, or bisexual may be blessed as infants and baptized in the Church without First Presidency approval. Additionally, the Church would "no longer characterize same-gender marriage by a Church member as 'apostasy'

---

12. *General Handbook: Serving in The Church of Jesus Christ of Latter-day Saints*, 32.6.3.2, ChurchofJesusChrist.org.

13. See Sarah Jane Weaver, "Policy Changes Announced for Members in Gay Marriages, Children of LGBT Parents," *Church News*, Apr. 4, 2019.

for purposes of Church discipline, although it is still considered 'a serious transgression'."[14]

Additionally, the Church provided guidance for transgender individuals and instructed that they "should be treated with sensitivity, kindness, compassion, and an abundance of Christlike love. All are welcome to attend sacrament meeting, other Sunday meetings, and social events of the Church. . . . If a [transgender] member decides to change his or her preferred name or pronouns of address, the name preference may be noted in the preferred name field on the membership record. The person may be addressed by the preferred name in the ward."[15] President Dallin H. Oaks explained, "Our members' efforts to show more understanding, compassion, and love should increase respect and understanding among all people of good will. We want to reduce the hate and contention so common today. We are optimistic that a majority of people—whatever their beliefs and orientations—long for better understanding and less contentious communications. That is surely our desire, and we seek the help of our members and others to attain it."[16]

In retrospect, one might ask: Was the member who questioned the policy right? Was the bishop wrong? Was the Church wrong? The short answer is no. The First Presidency did what the Lord wanted them to do when the Lord wanted them to do it. The bishop would have acted according to the Church's policy, his integrity, his wisdom, and the revelation he received. And the member would have acted in love and compassion. All were right; they were just not in sync. The Church of Jesus Christ of Latter-day Saints is like a large ship. It turns slowly at the command of the Captain. At times, those in the ship

---

14. Weaver, "Policy Changes Announced."

15. *General Handbook: Serving in The Church of Jesus Christ of Latter-day Saints*, 38.6.23, ChurchofJesusChrist.org.

16. Weaver, "Policy Changes Announced."

may want it to turn more quickly, but they must wait for the Captain to give the command, for the crew to understand and execute the command, and for the vessel to make the gradual turn.

In the same way, when we are in the Senior stage of faith, we may be out of sync with our leaders, the Church, and its policies. As in the Adult stage, we may not fit in just as Jesus did not fit in with His church.

CRISIS AT THE SENIOR STAGE

In the Senior stage, not fitting into the Church does not cause a crisis of faith as it did in the Adult stage. We are too full of love, too close to the Savior and our Father in Heaven, and unconcerned with the approval of others. We are equally unconcerned with our self-serving needs on Maslow's hierarchy—Physiological, Safety, Social, Esteem, and Self-Actualization—because we have achieved spiritual Transcendence. For this reason, we are not prone to experience a crisis of faith because we are content even if our self-serving needs are unsatisfied. Our only desire is to serve God and others. The challenge is staying in the Senior stage. We may simply drift to earlier stages as needed or when desired and then return to the Senior stage.

KEY POINT SUMMARY

- In the Senior stage of faith, we demonstrate unconditional love.
- There is only one commandment: thou shalt love.
- Transcendence is the highest level of development.
- We may be out of sync with the Church or its leaders and policies.

9

THE HOME STAGE
AND REGRESSION

"God not only sees where you are, He sees where you can be."

—Joyce Meyer[1]

As we conclude our discussion on the stages of faith, let us consider a few final points.

HOME STAGE

First, each of us has a home stage. Some have two home stages that are equally prevalent.[2] Much of our lives we will be in or returning to our home stage(s). My home stage is the Young Adult stage. I enjoy being anxiously engaged in the work. So, as I emerged from the dark night, I returned to the Young Adult stage. I returned to that

---

1. Joyce Meyer, "God not only sees," AZ Quotes, accessed Nov. 9, 2022, https://www.azquotes.com/quote/662612.

2. Janet O. Hagberg and Robert A. Guelich, *The Critical Journey: Stages in the Life of Faith* (Salem, WI: Sheffield Publishing Company, 2005), 9.

stage because it was familiar and invigorating. I just needed to return to my comfort zone long enough to catch my breath and regain my balance.

At the time, I didn't know I was regressing because I had not yet learned about the stages of faith. My intent was to return to full activity in the Church. I never stopped attending Church meetings, but I was an active-inactive—active on the outside but less active on the inside. I did all that my callings required of me, helped occasionally with service activities, and made appearances at various events, but I was not anxiously engaged, fully committed, or practicing the spiritual disciplines (e.g., reading scriptures, praying). As I again began to magnify my callings and found more opportunities to serve, there was a marked difference in me. I felt less comfortable drawing attention to myself and a greater concern for those around me. My dark night had transformed me.

As I was just emerging from my dark night, Jamie Turner, a friend who was in the depths of her own dark night, introduced me to the stages of faith. Suddenly, all that I had experienced made sense as I understood I had just passed through an essential stage of my spiritual journey. I then realized I had regressed to the Young Adult stage, and even though I was content in my home stage of faith, I knew I was just visiting.

Gradually, I took tentative steps into the Adult stage and began my inward journey. My journey inward instilled in me the desire to help others through their dark night and write this book. I began reading various works about the stages of faith and the dark night of the soul. Then I began my outward journey and started to write.

As I near completing this book, I am still in my outward journey with a long way to go. I have developed greater love, compassion, and selflessness, but there still remains a great measure of selfishness in me that is yet to be purged and a depth of love I have yet to develop. I imagine I will remain in the Adult stage for years, perhaps the remainder of my life, before I have developed sufficient love to transition to the Senior stage.

Regression

The second point is that we progress through the stages of faith in order but can regress in any order. Once we have passed through a stage, we can return to it at any time. We may return to previous stages when the stage we are in is difficult or when we want to experience the benefits of a previous stage.

For example, I regressed to the Young Adult stage because I wanted to feel valued and needed again. As I became more anxiously engaged in the work, leaders and other members of my ward recognized my efforts and appreciated my contribution. It felt good . . . but it was selfish. After my dark night and learning about the stages of faith, I became acutely aware of my self-serving nature and recognized that my return to the Young Adult stage was an act of selfishness. This taught me that we sometimes return to previous stages for selfish reasons. Then we repent and return to the stage the Lord intended for us.

At other times, we return to a previous stage to help others where they are. Paulien noted:

> We are attracted to people who are one stage ahead of us. We are perplexed by people who are two stages ahead of us. And people who get three stages ahead sometimes get killed (Jesus Christ). So effective mentoring occurs when the mentor willingly goes back a stage or two in order to meet people where they are (at stages one, two or three). This is not hypocrisy, it is recognizing that people learn best when the information is in a form they are prepared to handle (John 16:12), which is usually at most one stage ahead of

where they are at the moment. Moving backwards for the sake of others is an act of grace, not selfishness. It is an act of mission.[3]

No Hierarchy

Third, as explained earlier, one stage is not higher or better than another. The best and highest stage is the stage the Lord wants us in at the present time. A stage becomes better or higher only when we have become stagnant in our present stage or regressed to a previous stage to escape the stage the Lord intended for us.

Multiple Dark Nights

Finally, just as we can regress to previous stages, we can also regress back into the dark night. Some experience the dark night as a single, significant event. For them, it can be an overwhelming, debilitating, life-changing experience. Others may experience a dark night multiple times, sometimes in increasing intensity. Some have many dark nights. For them, each may be a mildly taxing experience that occurs repeatedly throughout their lives. Like waves over a rock, the dark nights come again and again, gradually wearing down their resolve. Every spiritual journey is different, and our heavenly parents tailor ours for our good and benefit.

Key Point Summary

- Each of us has a home stage.
- We progress through the stages in order but can regress in any order.

---

3. Jon Paulien, "The Stages of Faith," The Battle of Armageddon, accessed Nov. 10, 2022, http://thebattleofarmageddon.com/stages_of_faith.html.

- One stage is not better or higher than another.
- We may experience multiple dark nights of varying degrees of severity.

10

MENTORING

"As aspiring Christians but still imperfect Saints, we may not always understand the struggles of others or know how to help. But we can always love them, creating safe spaces where others—and often we ourselves—can struggle with the hard sayings in life."

—Eric D. Huntsman[1]

We should seek mentors through all the stages of faith. Mentors should be those who are at least one stage ahead of us. They should be able to explain the stages of faith and help us gain insight into what is happening at our current stage and help us see what is to happen next.

You should also be a mentor. If you have read this far, you are now equipped with the knowledge to help others on their spiritual journey. If you have personally experienced a crisis of faith, you may be able to recognize when others are in crises. Even if you have not experienced a crisis yourself, you may be gifted with the ability to sense it in others.

---

1. Eric D. Huntsman, "Hard Sayings and Safe Spaces: Making Room for Struggle as Well as Faith" (Brigham Young University devotional, Aug. 7, 2018), 2, speeches.byu.edu.

You may sense it when they walk into the chapel or ask questions in Sunday School.

Listen, love, and empathize without judgement. In the January 2011 *Ensign*, there is an article by Ann E. Tanner titled "Carrying Others to the Pool of Bethesda." In it, she explains, "Often, what is needed most is for us to be prayerful and to listen without giving advice or platitudes. People who are suffering don't need our explanation for their condition. Our well-meaning attempts to put the situation in perspective (our perspective) can unintentionally come across as demeaning or insensitive."[2]

Meet people where they are, as they are, and accept them for who they are. They may be steeped in sin. If so, love them and testify of the cleansing power of Christ's atonement and that the angels rejoice more over one soul that repents more than ninety-nine who require no repentance (see Luke 15:7). They may be bound by the chains of addiction. If so, love them and promise them that Christ can free them. They may be confused by events in Church history and angry at the Church for concealing those things, or perhaps they disagree with certain doctrines. If so, love them and empathize by expressing that you understand how those things can be confusing and upsetting, and offer to help them seek answers for their concerns when they are ready. They may be discouraged and filled with shame and self-loathing. If so, love them and remind them of their infinite worth to their Heavenly Father, for "God so loved the world, he gave his only begotten Son, that whosoever believeth in him should not perish, but have everlasting life" (John 3:16). Remind them that even if they were the only person to ever live on this earth, their heavenly parents still would have sent their Son to die for them.

---

2. Ann E. Tanner, "Carrying Others to the Pool of Bethesda," *Ensign*, Jan. 2011, 64–65.

Offer to walk with them on this journey, to be there for them, to listen, and to support them. You don't need to have all the answers. You just need to provide a safe space so they can explore their questions. Elder M. Russell Ballard said:

> I am concerned when I hear of sincere people asking honest questions about our history, doctrine, or practices and then being treated as though they were faithless. This is not the Lord's way. As Peter said, "Be ready always to give an answer to every man [or woman] that asketh you a reason of the hope that is in you" (1 Peter 3:15).
>
> We need to do better in responding to honest questions. Although we may not be able to answer every question about the cosmos or about our history, doctrine, and practices, we can provide many answers to those who are sincere. When we don't know the answer, we can search answers together—a shared search that may bring us closer to each other and closer to God.[3]

Share what you have learned about crises of faith when you teach, bear your testimony, or comment in classes. If you have personally endured the dark night, be vulnerable and share your experience and what you learned. As those who are in the depths of a crisis sense that you understand, they will trust that you may be able to help them and will come to you.

As they share, demonstrate that you are listening. Frequently echo what they are saying in your own words so they know you hear and understand them. State what you perceive they may be feeling so they know you empathize with them. You can say something like, "That must have been painful for you," or, "I can see how that would be confusing." Resist the impulse to share similar experiences from your life as a way to empathize with them. Sharing your stories makes the conversation about you. The best mentors focus the conversation on the person they are mentoring. Instead of sharing your stories, encourage

---

3. M. Russell Ballard, "An Epistle from an Apostle," *Liahona*, Sept. 2019.

the other person to continue to share, then share your own experiences when they are ready to listen. Teach them what you have learned about the stages of faith and the crises that help us transition to the next stage of our spiritual development.

Your objective as a mentor is to help them transition to the next stage, not to help them feel content in their current stage. If they become complacent in their current stage, they may again become stagnant and again experience a crisis of faith.

KEY POINT SUMMARY

- We should seek mentors.
- We should mentor others.
- When mentoring, we should listen, love, and empathize without judgement.

11

STAGES OF FAITH AND
MORAL DEVELOPMENT

*"In the end, we are all pilgrims seeking God's light as we journey on
the path of discipleship. We do not condemn others for the amount of
light they may or may not have; rather, we nourish and encourage all
light until it grows clear, bright, and true."*

—President Dieter F. Uchtdorf[1]

The stages of faith can be mapped to the stages of moral development. Lawrence Kohlberg developed a theory of moral development in 1958.[2] His theory focused specifically on the reasoning *process* that occurs when one considers a moral dilemma, rather than the final *decision* one makes.[3]

---

1. Dieter F. Uchtdorf, "Receiving a Testimony of Light and Truth," *Ensign* or *Liahona*, Nov. 2014, 22.

2. Lawrence Kohlberg, "The Development of Modes of Thinking and Choices in Years 10 to 16," PhD diss., (University of Chicago, 1958).

3. C. E. Sanders, "Lawrence Kohlberg's stages of moral development," *Encyclopedia Britannica*, Aug. 21, 2022, https://www.britannica.com/science/Lawrence-Kohlbergs-stages-of-moral-development.

He sought to understand how moral reasoning evolves as a person ages. To explore this, he selected a sample of seventy-two boys from Chicago whose ages ranged from ten to sixteen.[4] He presented each with various moral dilemmas and asked them to explain what they believed was the right thing to do and why.

One of the best known dilemmas was the Heinz story. Heinz's wife was dying of a certain form of cancer. There was a new drug discovered by a local chemist that the doctors believed could cure her. Heinz went to the chemist to purchase the drug, but the chemist wanted to charge Heinz ten times more than it cost to produce the drug, an amount Heinz could not afford. Heinz sought help from family and friends but was only able to raise half the funds required to purchase the drug. He went to the chemist and explained that his wife was dying and he needed the drug to save her life. He offered the chemist all the money he had raised and asked him if he would accept what he could afford to pay or allow him to pay the remainder later. The chemist refused. Desperate to save his wife, later that night the husband broke into the chemist's lab and stole the drug.[5]

Kohlberg then asked the boys a series of questions like these:

- Should Heinz have stolen the drug?
- Would it change anything if Heinz did not love his wife?
- What if the person dying was a stranger? Would it make any difference?
- Should the police arrest the chemist for murder if the woman died?

---

4. See Lawrence Kohlberg, *The Psychology of Moral Development: The Nature and Validity of Moral Stages (Essays on Moral Development, Volume 2)* (New York City: Harper & Row, 1984),

5. Saul McLeod, "Kohlberg's Theory of Moral Development," Simply Psychology, last updated 2013, https://www.simplypsychology.org/kohlberg.html.

Kohlberg was not so concerned with what the boys believed was right or wrong; he was more interested in the reasons for their decisions. He discovered that older boys used different reasoning than younger boys. He then concluded that humans pass through three levels of moral development, which he subdivided into six stages:

Level 1: Pre-Conventional morality – Authority figures define what is right and wrong.

Stage 1: Obedience and Punishment Orientation – We act morally to avoid punishment.

Stage 2: Individualism and Exchange – We recognize that different authority figures have different opinions of what is right and wrong. We act morally out of self-interest; we obey expecting the authority figure to reward us.

Level 2: Conventional morality – Social norms and rules define right and wrong.

Stage 3: Good Interpersonal Relationships – We want to fit into our social group and want others to think of us as good people. We also develop concern for others.

Stage 4: Maintaining Social Order – We recognize how our individual behavior affects the overall community and believe it is best for all to follow the rules and obey authority figures to maintain order and prevent chaos.

Level 3: Post-Conventional morality – Universal ethical principles define right and wrong (e.g., sanctity of life, equality, justice, dignity).

Stage 5: Social Contract and Individual Rights – We measure moral issues against our personal values, consider them from a wholistic perspective, and recognize that social norms and laws may not be just in all circumstances. We see there are times when what is right for an individual supersedes what the community considers right.

Stage 6: Universal Principles – We live according to our personal values regardless of the laws and societal norms. We do what is right because it is the right thing to do and may publicly fight against perceived injustice, even at the risk of imprisonment, injury, or death.[6]

Here is a succinct table of Kohlberg's model.

	Why We Do What's Right	Opinion about Others
Stage 1	We fear punishment	Authority figures define what is right and wrong
Stage 2	We want to be rewarded	People have different opinions of right and wrong
Stage 3	We want others to like us	We should care for others
Stage 4	We want to prevent chaos	All must maintain social order
Stage 5	It is the right thing to do	Society should be equitable for all
Stage 6	We cannot tolerate injustice	Society must change to be equitable for all

Now let us consider the Heinz dilemma to illustrate moral reasoning at each stage. If someone were asked, "If you were Heinz, would you have stolen the drug?" the person may offer responses like these depending on which stage of moral development they were in.

Stage 1: I would not have stolen the drug because it is wrong to steal. Stealing is illegal, and I would not want to go to jail.

Stage 2: I believe it would be right to steal the drug, though the chemist would disagree.

Stage 3: I would steal the drug to care for my wife.

Stage 4: I would not have stolen the drug because it is illegal to steal. If everyone stole, it would cause chaos.

Stage 5: I would have stolen the drug because my wife would die without it, and the laws do not account for such circumstances.

---

6. Serhat Kurt, "Stages of Moral Development – Lawrence Kohlberg," Educational Technology, Aug. 17, 2020, https://educationaltechnology.net/stages-of-moral-development-lawrence-kohlberg/.

Stage 6: I would have stolen the drug because the value of one's life supersedes the value of one's property.

Note how each stage represents a gradual transition from selfishness to selflessness, self-serving to serving, caring for self to caring for others, intolerance to tolerance, and blind obedience to moral reasoning.

We experience a parallel progression as we transition through the stages of faith. In the Child stage of faith, we fear punishment and desire blessings. We do what is right because it is good for us. Our motives are self-serving. In the Adolescent stage of faith, we want to fit into our Church community. Again, our motives are self-serving. In the Young Adult stage of faith, we want to be a valued member of the community and do what's best for the community. We are still self-serving but transitioning to a serving mindset. In the Adult stage of faith, our evolving love for others leads us to do what is best for others. At this stage, we are more serving than self-serving. Finally, in the Senior stage of faith, our love causes us to be self-sacrificing, and we do the right thing because it is the right thing to do.

Stages of Faith	Stages of Moral Development	Maslow's Needs	Why We Do What's Right
Child Stage	We fear punishment and desire blessings	Physiological/Safety	It's good for us
Adolescent Stage	We want to be liked and fit in	Social	
Young Adult Stage	We contribute to the community	Esteem	It's good for us and others
Adult Stage	We have a deep love for others	Self-Actualization	It's good for others
Senior Stage	We sacrifice all for others	Transcendence	It's the right thing to do

Collective Progression

Now let us shift from discussing individual progression to discussing collective progression. Here we will explore the moral evolution of God's people and their progress through the stages of faith. We will observe that the people of God spent millennia stagnant in the Child stage of faith before collectively transitioning into the Adolescent stage. Once they were in the Adolescent stage, they stagnated again until the Lord helped His followers transition to higher stages of faith. We will see how the Lord modified His methods to fit the people's level of moral development. This will explain why the Lord, who is "the same yesterday, and today, and forever" (Hebrews 13:8), evolves from being wrathful and vengeful to loving and kind.

Old Testament Times

Since the fall of Adam, our Father in Heaven has been guiding His people through the stages of faith and moral development. Like any loving parent, He guides us with rules and modifies those rules as our ability to govern ourselves increases. Consider how parents change the rules as their child matures. When a child is a toddler, the parents require the child to stay in the house. Then, as the child matures, the child can leave the house but must stay in the yard. Then the child learns how to ride a bike and can leave the yard but must stay in the neighborhood. Then, as a teen, the child can go with friends but must be home by a defined curfew. Finally, as a young adult, the parents allow the child to decide where to go and when to come home. The parents did not change—they only modified the restrictions on the child as the child changed. In the same way, our Father in Heaven initially gives us restrictive commandments that He gradually modifies as we mature spiritually and morally. Though He is unchanging, He modifies how He leads us to fit our level of development.

When Adam and Eve were cast out of the Garden of Eden, the Lord commanded them to "offer the firstlings of their flocks, for an offering unto the Lord. And Adam was obedient unto the commandments of the Lord. And after many days an angel of the Lord appeared unto Adam, saying: Why dost thou offer sacrifices unto the Lord? And Adam said unto him: I know not, save the Lord commanded me" (Moses 5:5–6). Adam was in the first stage of moral development and the Child stage of faith. He was in awe of God and submitted entirely to His will. Adam relied on the Lord as the authority figure to define the rules, and Adam obeyed.

Adam and Eve "blessed the name of God" (Moses 5:12) and continued to obey the Lord. They taught their children the gospel (see Moses 5:12), but their children "believed it not, and they loved Satan more than God. And men began from that time forth to be carnal, sensual, and devilish" (Moses 5:13). Adam lived 930 years, and during that time most of his children descended into ever-increasing wickedness.

Enoch was born when Adam was about 642 years old.[7] The Lord spoke to Enoch and said:

> Enoch, my son, prophesy unto this people, and say unto them— Repent, for thus saith the Lord: I am angry with this people, and my fierce anger is kindled against them; for their hearts have waxed hard, and their ears are dull of hearing, and their eyes cannot see afar off.
>
> And for these many generations, ever since the day that I created them, have they gone astray, and have denied me, and have sought their own counsels in the dark; and in their own abominations have

---

7. "Bible Timeline: Chronological Index of the Years and Times from Adam unto Christ," HBU, accessed Nov. 7, 2022, https://hbu.edu/museums/dunham-bible-museum/tour-of-the-museum/bible-in-america/bibles-for-a-young-republic/chronological-index-of-the-years-and-times-from-adam-unto-christ/.

they devised murder, and have not kept the commandments, which I gave unto their father, Adam.

Wherefore, they have foresworn themselves, and, by their oaths, they have brought upon themselves death; and a hell I have prepared for them, if they repent not; (Moses 6:27–29)

Go to this people, and say unto them—Repent, lest I come out and smite them with a curse, and they die. (Moses 7:10)

Note how the Lord threatened them with a curse, death, and hell if they would not repent. The people were at the lowest level of moral development, and the Lord knew that fear of punishment would cause them to repent and come unto Him.

Enoch did as the Lord commanded, and the people repented and established a righteous city. "And the Lord called his people Zion, because they were of one heart and one mind, and dwelt in righteousness; and there was no poor among them" (Moses 7:18). The city of Enoch transitioned to the Senior stage of faith and the highest stage of moral development and "in process of time, was taken up into heaven" (Moses 7:21).

Noah was Enoch's great-grandson. The Lord sent Noah to warn the people that if they did not repent, He would "send in floods upon them" (Moses 8:17). Notice again that the people were at the lowest level of moral development; therefore, the Lord sought to save them by threatening punishment.

But "the wickedness of men had become great in the earth; and every man was lifted up in the imagination of the thoughts of his heart, being only evil continually" (Moses 8:22). "And they hearkened not unto the words of Noah" (Moses 8:21). The Lord commanded Noah to build the ark (see Genesis 1:14) to save his family and selected animals from the flood. Then the Lord caused the flood and destroyed every "man, and beast, and the creeping thing, and the fowls of the air" (Genesis 6:7) that were not in the ark.

Noah lived 950 years and died around the time Abram (Abraham) was born. Abraham begat Isaac, who begat Jacob (Israel). Jacob's sons sold Joseph, their younger brother, into slavery. Joseph later ascended from prisoner to second-in-command in Egypt and saved Egypt and his family from a great famine. Pharaoh honored Joseph for saving Egypt and invited his family to reside in Egypt.

Over time, the Egyptians forgot Joseph's service to Egypt. Jacob's descendants, the Hebrews, became so numerous that the Egyptians were concerned they would collude with Egypt's enemies and rise up against them. To quell their fears, the Egyptians enslaved the Hebrews. When the Hebrews continued to multiply, Pharaoh ordered that every male born to the Hebrews should be killed.

Moses was born to Hebrew slaves. His mother, seeking to save his life, set him in an ark she made from bulrushes and tar and floated him down the Nile River. Pharaoh's daughter, who was bathing in the river, found Moses and raised him as her own son, as a prince in Egypt.

When Moses was an adult, he saw an Egyptian beating a Hebrew slave. Incensed by the burdens the Egyptians had placed on his people, he killed the Egyptian. The next day, he learned that someone had witnessed the murder. He then fled to Midian, fearing that Pharoah would slay him.

Moses lived in Midian for about forty years. Then the Lord appeared to him on Mount Horeb and commanded him to bring the children of Israel out of Egypt. Moses returned to Egypt and warned Pharaoh of ten plagues that would come upon him and his people if he would not allow the Hebrews to leave. Again, note the threat of punishment as the means of leading Pharaoh to obey the Lord. The Egyptians were also at the lowest stage of moral development.

Eventually, Pharaoh let the Hebrews go. They departed into the wilderness, and "the Lord went before them by day in a pillar of a cloud, to lead them the way; and by night in a pillar of fire, to give them light; to go by day and night" (Exodus 13:21). Pharaoh and his army pursued the Hebrews who were trapped against the Red Sea. As the Egyptians approached, the Lord instructed Moses to part the sea, and the Hebrews fled through it on dry ground to the other side. The Egyptians chased after them and were swallowed up as the sea closed in around them. Moses and the Hebrews then began their journey to Canaan, the promised land.

The Lord brought them to gates of the promised land in eleven days (see Deuteronomy 1:2), but the people of Israel would wander in the wilderness for another forty years. Why? Because they were overcome with doubt—a collective crisis of faith.

When they were within sight of the promised land, Moses sent spies to survey the area. They returned after forty days and reported that the land was flowing with milk and honey and had much fruit, but the cities were walled and the people were strong and the men were giants (see Numbers 13:33). Hearing that report, the Hebrews fell into despair. They "lifted up their voice, and cried; and . . . wept that night" (Numbers 14:1). They murmured that God should have just let them die in Egypt or in the wilderness. They then begged to return to Egypt because it seemed better to them to be slaves than to die in war at the gates of the promised land.

It is perplexing that a people who had seen so many miracles could be filled with so much doubt. They had witnessed the ten plagues. The Lord had led them with a pillar of fire. They had faced one of most powerful leaders and armies of the time with no training, no armor, and no weapons, and yet through the power of God, they were victorious without the loss of a single soul. How could they now question His ability to give them the promised land? They were filled with doubt because the Lord was pressing them into the next stage of faith, the next stage of their moral development.

They had faith. They prayed that God would deliver them from the Egyptians (see Exodus 2:23), and the Lord sent Moses in answer to their prayers (see Exodus 2:24–25). But they were in the Child stage, desiring safety and security and life-sustaining needs beyond the meager amounts meted out by their captors. Obedience was forced upon them by their taskmasters, so they were incapable of governing themselves. Now the Lord wanted them to progress to the next stage of faith, but they, like most of us, balked and were overcome with doubts.

The Lord asked Moses and Aaron, "How long shall I bear with this evil congregation, which murmur against me?" (Numbers 14:27). He then decreed that the people would wander in the wilderness for forty years until all that were then twenty years or older were dead. Their children and Caleb and Joshua, who had not murmured against Him, would inherit the promised land.

The Lord was angry with the people (see Doctrine and Covenants 84:24), but He was not surprised. He knew they would murmur and doubt before He brought them to the gates of the promised land. Yet He brought them anyway. Why? Because He was pressing them to move to the next stage of faith and moral development. Sometimes the Lord brings us to the gates of our promised land knowing they are locked to us—knowing it will cause disappointment and despair. He does this

We develop greater faith after we have endured discouragement, doubt, and despair.

because we develop greater faith after we have endured discouragement, doubt, and despair, "for ye receive no witness until after the trial of your faith" (see Ether 12:6).

The Israelites then began their forty-year sojourn in the wilderness. About forty-five days after leaving Egypt,[8] the Lord instructed Moses to prepare the people because He would appear to them (see Exodus 33:11). Most of the people sanctified themselves as Moses instructed, and on the morning of the third day, they gathered at Mount Sanai to see Jehovah. But apparently too many were unprepared. The Lord refused to reveal Himself to them, lest "many of them perish" (Exodus 19:21). Moses then went up into the mount to receive the "tables of stone, and a law, and commandments" (Exodus 24:12) written by the finger of the Lord. Eleven chapters of the Book of Exodus (chapters 20–23, 25–31)—a total of 369 verses—record what the Lord said to Moses. Almost all these verses comprise restrictive commandments, rules, and orders. Clearly, the people were at the Child stage of faith and the lowest level of moral development—they required explicit instructions that left little room for interpretation or confusion.

Moses communed with the Lord for forty days and nights (see Exodus 24:18). The people, fearing Moses was dead, begged Aaron to make them a god. He collected their gold, melted it, and formed a molten calf. The people worshipped the calf, declaring, "These be thy gods, O Israel, which brought thee up out of the land of Egypt" (Exodus 32:4). Then they reveled in idolatrous immorality.

The Lord was angry with them and threatened to consume them (see Exodus 32:10). Moses assuaged the Lord's anger and descended the mount to chastise the people. When he beheld their depravity, he cast down the tables of stone, shattering them. He destroyed the idol and ordered the execution of three thousand men (see Exodus 32:27–28). "The Lord plagued the people, because they made the calf" (Exodus 32:35), but Moses instructed them to consecrate themselves unto the Lord that He may bless them (see Exodus 32:29). Notice the

---

8. See "Exodus 19:1: Clarke's Commentary," Study Light, accessed Nov. 10, 2022, https://www.studylight.org/commentary/exodus/19-1.html.

use of punishment and reward. The men were executed and the people were plagued, but they were also promised blessings if they would dedicate themselves to the Lord. This is additional evidence that the people were at the lowest level of moral development.

The Lord then instructed Moses to hew two new tables of stone. The Lord inscribed upon those tables the words of the law, just as they were written on the first tables. However, He took the Holy Priesthood, the higher ordinances, and eventually their prophet from the people and gave them the law of carnal commandments (see Doctrine and Covenants 84:23–27; Joseph Smith Translation, Exodus 34:1–2 [in Exodus 34, footnote *a*]). The word *carnal* relates to the desires of the flesh. Therefore, the law of carnal commandments governed physical desires (e.g., lust, greed, gluttony, envy, sloth, pride). Abinadi, as he stood before King Noah, explained why the Lord took the higher laws and ordinances from Israel and gave them only the law of carnal commandments:

> And now I say unto you that it was expedient that there should be a law given to the children of Israel, yea, even a very strict law; for they were a stiffnecked people, quick to do iniquity, and slow to remember the Lord their God;
>
> Therefore there was a law given them, yea, a law of performances and of ordinances, a law which they were to observe strictly from day to day, to keep them in remembrance of God and their duty towards him. (Mosiah 13:29–30)

After the Lord gave the commandments recorded in the eleven chapters of Exodus, He then proceeded to give Moses additional commandments recorded in Leviticus and Deuteronomy. Leviticus comprises twenty-seven chapters (859 verses) of meticulous and tedious rules and regulations. In total, the Lord gave Moses 613 commandments.[9] It is evident that the more stiffnecked and iniquitous the people are, the more the Lord increases the number of restrictive commandments and decreases revelation. Conversely, as His people become more godly, revelations increase and commandments decrease. In other words, the more apt we are to do what is right, the less apt He is to restrict our actions with carnal commandments and the more apt He is to guide us with revelation.

John Taylor said that a member of legislature once asked Joseph Smith how it was that he was able to "govern so many people, and to preserve such perfect order; remarking at the same time that it was impossible for them to do it anywhere else. Mr. Smith remarked that it was very easy to do that. 'How?' responded the gentleman; 'to us it is very difficult.' Mr. Smith replied, 'I teach them correct principles, and they govern themselves.'"[10] The more we learn to live by correct principles, the more the Lord permits us to govern ourselves.

As God's people become more godly, revelations increase and commandments decrease.

It is not the Lord's desire to burden us with numerous, restrictive commandments. He has said, "For behold, it is not meet that I should command in all things; for he that is compelled in all things, the same is a slothful and not a wise servant; wherefore he receiveth no reward. Verily I say, men should be anxiously engaged in a good cause, and do many things of their own free will, and bring to pass much righteousness" (Doctrine and Covenants 58:26–27).

---

9. See "A List of the 613 Mitzvot (Commandments)," Judaism 101, accessed Nov. 10, 2022, https://www.jewfaq.org/613.htm.

10. John Taylor, "The Organization of the Church," *Millennial Star*, Nov. 15, 1851, 339.

He desires for us to progress through the stages of moral development so it becomes unnecessary for Him to "command in all things." In fact, the reason we have so many commandments is because we cannot keep the one great commandment: *thou shalt love.* As explained earlier, if we

> *The more we learn to live by correct principles, the more the Lord permits us to govern ourselves.*

could simply learn to love perfectly, there would be no need for any carnal commandments (see Romans 13:8–13; Matthew 22:37–39).

Jesus' Time

Now we will move forward from Moses's time to Jesus' mortal ministry. Specifically, we will consider the collective level of moral development of the people of His day. As explained earlier, the Pharisees and Sadducees were in the Adolescent and Young Adult stages of faith and still in the lower stages of moral development. They did what was right to gratify their pride and to maintain social order. Since they were the religious leaders of that time, the people of God collectively practiced strict obedience to the law and were therefore in the Child and Adolescent stages of faith and the first stages of moral development.

Jesus wanted the Pharisees and Sadducees to transition from the Adolescent and Young Adult stages to the Adult Stage. This is evident from the fact that He continually taught and modeled the gospel of love (see Matthew 22:37–39). At the Last Supper, Jesus said to his disciples, "A new commandment I give unto you, That ye love one another; as I have loved you, that ye also love one another" (John 13:34). The commandment to love was not a new commandment. In fact, it was in the original law of Moses in Deuteronomy 6:5 and Leviticus 19:18. The Pharisees and Sadducees knew this. When the lawyer asked Jesus what he must do to inherit eternal life, Jesus asked him, "What is written in the law?" The lawyer replied, "Thou shalt love the Lord thy God with all thy heart, and with all thy soul, and with all thy strength, and with all thy mind; and thy neighbour as thyself." Then Jesus responded, "Thou hast answered right: this do, and thou shalt live" (Luke 10:26–28).

At another time, a different lawyer asked Jesus, "Master, which is the great commandment in the law? Jesus said unto him, Thou shalt love the Lord thy God with all thy heart, and with all thy soul, and with all thy mind. This is the first and great commandment. And the second is like unto it, Thou shalt love thy neighbour as thyself. On these two commandments hang all the law and the prophets" (Matthew 22:36–40). The lawyer then replied, "Well, Master, thou hast said the truth: for there is one God; and there is none other but he: And to love him with all the heart, and with all the understanding, and with all the soul, and with all the strength, and to love his neighbour as himself, is more than all whole burnt offerings and sacrifices" (Mark 12:32–33).

Clearly, the commandment to love was not a new commandment. What *was* new was the degree of love the commandment called for: to love as Jesus loved. He explained, "Greater love hath no man than this, that a man lay down his life for his friends" (John 15:13).

The Pharisees and Sadducees knew the law of love but somehow disregarded it among all the "thou shalts" and "thou shalt nots." To counteract this, Jesus continually taught and demonstrated love to a degree that was absurd to them. He befriended publicans and sinners (see Luke 15:1–2). He was kind to Samaritans (see John 4:7–27). He touched the outcast lepers (see Matthew 8:3). He healed the blind, lame, and deaf (see Luke 7:22), even though the Jews believed their maladies were God's punishment for sins (see John 9:2). He declared that the angels rejoice more over one sinner who repents than ninety-nine righteous who require no repentance (see Luke 15:7–10). The

Pharisees and Sadducees were rightfully offended by His implication that God loved repentant sinners more than He loved them in their self-righteousness. His love of the disenfranchised bewildered them, and His subtle criticism infuriated them (see Luke 20:19, 46–47).

Notice how they attempted to trap Jesus between love and the law when they brought to Him the woman caught in adultery. They said to Him, "Now Moses in the law commanded us, that such should be stoned: but what sayest thou?" (John 8:5). They calculated that His propensity for love and mercy would either cause Him to break the law of Moses (so they could accuse Him) or to subject Himself to the law (thus negating His message of love and mercy).

Instead, Jesus stooped down and began to write in the dirt with His finger. Ironically, this was the same finger that had inscribed on the tables of stone the very commandments they were now weaponizing against Him. We do not know what He wrote in the sand. Some have postulated that He wrote the sins of which her accusers were guilty. He then said to those who were gathered, "He that is without sin among you, let him first cast a stone at her" (John 8:7). Convicted by their consciences, they each walked away, leaving Jesus and the woman alone. With none left to accuse her, Jesus said, "Neither do I condemn thee: go, and sin no more" (John 8:11). He did not forgive her; rather, He instructed her to repent so she could obtain forgiveness. His actions demonstrated perfect love, mercy, and justice.

The Pharisees and Sadducees failed to transition from the Adolescent stage; however, the Church that Jesus established *did* transition to the Young Adult stage. The Pharisees and Sadducees eventually slew Jesus and each of the apostles except John (see Doctrine and Covenants 7:1–3). As a result, the Church fell into apostasy—its dark night of the soul.

PRESENT DAY

Now let us shift forward in time to the present day. Since the time of Christ's mortal ministry, Christians have gradually transitioned from the law of Moses nearer to the law of love. We no longer sentence someone to death if they work on the Sabbath (see Exodus 31:15) or commit adultery (see Leviticus 20:10). We do not stone rebellious teens (see Deuteronomy 21:18–21; Exodus 21:17). We have made great strides since the days of the Spanish Inquisition and the Salem witch trials. Even in the last fifty years, Christians have become less self-righteous, less judgmental, and more accepting of others, all of which are evidence of increasing love. Some denominations have become so accepting that they have appointed openly gay ministers,[11] a departure from what are considered traditional values of Christianity. Though we are increasing in love and acceptance of others, we are far from emulating the principles of perfect love outlined in the Sermon on the Mount.

Apparently, we have also progressed morally. In The Church of Jesus Christ of Latter-day Saints, there has been a shift from restrictive instruction to revelation, which is evidence of moral progression. As explained earlier, as we mature morally we become better at self-governance, and then commandments decrease and revelations increase. For example, in 1998, the Church introduced a new Church Handbook of Instructions that consisted of just two books: one for stake presidencies and bishoprics and another for priesthood and auxiliary leaders. The new handbooks replaced thirty-one previously used

---

11. See "First Openly Gay Minister to be Ordained by Presbyterian Church (USA) Tomorrow," National LGBTQ Task Force, accessed Nov. 10, 2022, https://www.thetaskforce.org/first-openly-gay-minister-to-be-ordained-by-presbyterian-church-usa-tomorrow/

publications.[12] In the introduction to the handbook, leaders were instructed to rely on revelation more than policy as they learn their duties in the Church. The Church has reprinted these same instructions in subsequent handbooks to the present day:

> The Lord taught, "Let every man learn his duty, and to act in the office in which he is appointed, in all diligence" (Doctrine and Covenants 107:99). As a leader in The Church of Jesus Christ of Latter-day Saints, you should seek personal revelation to help you learn and fulfill the duties of your calling.
>
> Studying the scriptures and the teachings of latter-day prophets will help you understand and fulfill your duties. As you study the words of God, you will be more receptive to the influence of the Spirit (see Doctrine and Covenants 84:85).
>
> You also learn your duties by studying the instructions in this handbook. These instructions can invite revelation if they are used to provide an understanding of principles, policies, and procedures to apply while seeking the guidance of the Spirit.[13]

Note the order of the instructions and the consistent message:

1. Seek personal revelation.
2. Study the scriptures and words of modern prophets to be more open to revelation from the Spirit.
3. Study the handbook to invite revelation and the guidance of the Spirit.

Also note that the emphasis is on receiving personal revelation, not following the rules and regulations outlined in the handbook. The Lord guides us very differently today than He did in the days of Moses. He has decreased commandments and increased revelation.

---

12. See *General Handbook: Serving in The Church of Jesus Christ of Latter-day Saints* (1998).

13. *General Handbook: Serving in The Church of Jesus Christ of Latter-day Saints*, 0.0, ChurchofJesusChrist.org.

Another example is in the missionary program. In 1961, the Church introduced a set of discussions, *A Uniform System for Teaching Investigators*.[14] The missionaries were instructed to memorize the discussions and quote them verbatim when teaching investigators. In 1986, the Church introduced a new set of discussions. They outlined the principles that missionaries were to teach, provided the order of instruction, and suggested scriptures and examples, but the missionaries were encouraged to "rely on the Spirit to decide what [would] be most helpful to each investigator."[15]

Today, the missionaries teach from *Preach My Gospel*. They are to follow the Spirit and have great flexibility to choose what and how they teach. The instructions in *Preach My Gospel* state, "You have the flexibility to teach the lessons in whatever way best helps people fully prepare for their baptism and confirmation . . . You can teach the lessons in many ways. Which lesson you teach, when you teach it, and how much time you give to it are best determined by the needs of the person you are teaching and the direction of the Spirit. Do not memorize the entire lesson."[16]

Again, we see the pattern of restrictive instructions paving the way for self-direction. The decrease in restrictive instructions and the increased reliance on revelation indicates the moral evolution of the missionaries and the Church as a whole.

One final note on this topic. Those at the highest stage of moral development transcend the commandments. Nephi's experience of obtaining the brass plates is a perfect example of this. Lehi had instructed Nephi and his brothers to obtain the brass plates from

---

14. See *A Uniform System for Teaching Investigators* (Salt Lake City: The Church of Jesus Christ of Latter-day Saints, 1961).

15. *A Uniform System for Teaching Investigators* (Salt Lake City: The Church of Jesus Christ of Latter-day Saints, 1986), 2.

16. *Preach My Gospel: A Guide to Missionary Service* (2018), viii–ix.

Laban. The brass plates were "the official scriptures"[17] of that time and contained the writings of some of the prophets found in the Old Testament as well as the writings of prophets we have no other record of (e.g., Zenos, Zenock, Neum, and Ezias).

Laman, the oldest brother, first attempted to obtain the plates by cordially asking Laban to give them to him. Laban was angry with Laman, accused him of attempted robbery, and threw him out, threatening to kill him (see 1 Nephi 3:11–13). Next, they gathered all their gold, silver, and precious possessions and offered them to Laban in exchange for the plates. Laban stole their property, cast them out, and sent his servants to kill them (see 1 Nephi 3:22–26).

They escaped and hid themselves. The older brothers, Laman and Lemuel, were faithless and frustrated. They murmured and beat their younger brothers with a rod until an angel appeared and censured them. Afterward, they continued to murmur (see 1 Nephi 3:28–31).

Finally, Nephi went to obtain the plates. He explained, "I was led by the Spirit, not knowing beforehand the things which I should do" (1 Nephi 4:6). Note his dependence on revelation and freedom from restrictive instructions. As Nephi approached Laban's house, he found Laban drunk and passed out on the ground. He drew Laban's sword as the Spirit whispered to him to slay Laban. Nephi refused. To slay Laban would have violated the commandment "thou shalt not kill," even though one could argue that Laban's actions warranted it. The Spirit insisted, explaining, "It is better that one man should perish than that a nation should dwindle and perish in unbelief" (1 Nephi 4:13). Nephi reasoned that Laban had stolen their possessions and attempted to kill them. Nephi also considered that his descendants needed the scriptures, and he knew that the Lord had delivered Laban

---

17. Sidney Branton Sperry, *Answers to Book of Mormon Questions* (Salt Lake City: Bookcraft, 1967), 43–44.

to him to obtain the plates. Nephi then slew Laban, not in violation of the command of God but in obedience to it.

Nephi's ability to perfectly respond to revelation transcended the written law and enabled him to obey the Lord's law in the moment. As the apostle Paul explained, "But if ye be led of the Spirit, ye are not under the law" (Galatians 5:18). This is the highest level of moral development—to do what is right because it is the right thing to do. Nephi had no fear of punishment and no hope for reward. He was not seeking to gratify his pride or maintain social order, nor was he driven by a sense of fairness. He simply wanted to do the right thing for the right reasons. Nephi was at the highest level of moral development. He transcended the written law and was led entirely by the Spirit.

The Church of Jesus Christ of Latter-day Saints

Now let us consider The Church of Jesus Christ of Latter-day Saints and discuss its stage of faith. Paulien stated that churches "reflect the spiritual stage that is the common denominator of the total membership. Since the vast majority of adherents to any religion would be in the earlier stages of faith, most religious institutions would be in stages one, two or three."[18] As previously noted, the Church has progressed morally as evidenced by increase in love and decrease in restrictive instructions. The community is strong, and members of the Church are anxiously engaged. These characteristics would indicate that the Church is in Stage 4 of moral development and the Young Adult stage of faith, and it is on the cusp of its dark night.

---

18. Jon Paulien, "The Stages of Faith," The Battle of Armageddon, accessed Nov. 10, 2022, http://thebattleofarmageddon.com/stages_of_faith.html.

The Coming Universal Dark Night

In Matthew 24, the Savior spoke of a severe universal dark night that will occur prior to his return. He warned there will be wars, famines, pestilences, and earthquakes (see verses 6–7). He prophesied that the followers of Christ will be hated, persecuted, and killed (see verse 9). Iniquity will abound and love will wax cold (see verse 12). There will be "great tribulation, such as was not since the beginning of the world to this time, no, nor ever shall be" (verse 21). And there will "arise false Christs, and false prophets, and shall shew great signs and wonders; insomuch that, if it were possible, they shall deceive the very elect" (verse 24).

"The elect are those who love God with all their hearts and live lives that are pleasing to Him."[19] They are the Lord's sheep who "hear [His] voice" (John 10:27), "harden not their hearts" (Doctrine and Covenants 29:7), and follow Him (see John 10:27). They are the strongest followers of Christ and will not be deceived during the universal dark night. But what of those who are not "very elect?" Those who are somewhat elect or not elect at all? Apparently, most will be deceived.

When the Lord returns, He will divide His sheep (those who follow Him) from the goats (those who do not follow Him) (see Matthew 25:31–34). It seems that a preliminary separating of the sheep and goats is already in progress. In 2020, Ronald F. Inglehart published an article in *Foreign Affairs* titled "Giving Up on God." In the article, he explained that since 1981, he and his colleagues have analyzed data on the religious trends of forty-nine countries representing 60 percent of the world population. Their data showed that, from 1981 to 2007, the people in thirty-three of the forty-nine countries "became more

---

19. Guide to the Scriptures, "Elect," scriptures.ChurchofJesusChrist.org.

religious during those years."[20] However, since 2007 there has been a significant change. Forty-three out of the forty-nine countries they studied—an overwhelming majority—have become less religious. Most significantly, the United States, which prior to 2007 ranked among the most religious countries, has plummeted to the eleventh least religious country of those surveyed, the most dramatic departure from religion of all the countries studied.

In 2021, the Pew Research Center conducted a national public opinion reference survey (NPORS). They "asked respondents how often they pray and how important religion is in their lives. Today, fewer than half of U.S. adults (45%) say they pray on a daily basis. By contrast, nearly six-in-ten (58%) reported praying daily in the 2007 Religious Landscape Study, as did 55% in the 2014 Landscape Study. Roughly one-third of U.S. adults (32%) now say they seldom or never pray, up from 18% who said this in 2007."[21]

Additionally, Americans are becoming less religious. In 2007, 56 percent of those surveyed said they were very religious. In 2021, only 41 percent claimed to be very religious.[22]

We see a similar departure from the faith among Latter-day Saints. Darren E. Sherkat, a professor of sociology, conducted a 2014 study of the major religions in the United States, including The Church of Jesus Christ of Latter-day Saints. He considered three criteria to measure religious affiliation and loyalty:

---

20. See Ronald F. Inglehart, "Giving Up on God: The Global Decline of Religion," *Foreign Affairs*, Sept. 2020, https://www.foreignaffairs.com/articles/world/2020-08-11/religion-giving-god.

21. Gregory A. Smith, "About Three-in-Ten U.S. Adults Are Now Religiously Unaffiliated," Pew Research Center, Dec. 14, 2021, https://www.pewforum.org/2021/12/14/about-three-in-ten-u-s-adults-are-now-religiously-unaffiliated/.

22. See Smith, "About Three-in-Ten U.S. Adults."

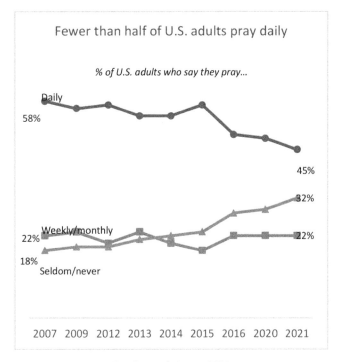

Pew Research Center, 2021

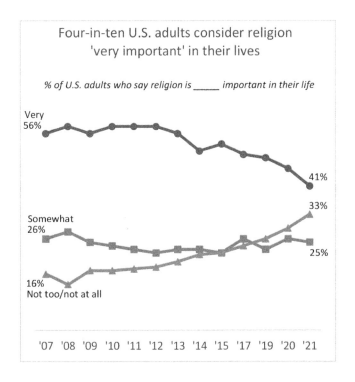

- *Religious Loyalty*: percentage of adults who continue to affiliate with the religion they professed at age sixteen
- *Religious Apostasy*: percentage of adults who left the religion they professed at age sixteen and are presently unaffiliated with a religion
- *Gains and Losses from Switching*: fluctuation in membership numbers based on the number of people joining and leaving a religion

He discovered that loyalty to the Church dropped 61 percent among those born between 1971 and 1994 as compared to prior generations, ranking Latter-day Saints among the least loyal groups in the youngest generation.[23] Jana Riess and Benjamin Knoll, Latter-day Saint scholars, reanalyzed Sherkat's data and discovered that religious loyalty dropped 46 percent among Latter-day Saint millennials (those born between 1981 and 1994).[24]

	Birth Years				
	Before 1925	**1925– 1943**	**1944– 1945**	**1956– 1970**	**1971– 1994**
Religious Loyalty	75.8%	74.2%	72.4%	71.2%	61.2%
Religious Apostasy	4.8%	5.8%	9.7%	17.6%	27.1%
Gains and Losses from Switching	29.0%	25.0%	21.0%	2.0%	-28.0%

23. See Darren E. Sherkat, *Changing Faith: The Dynamics and Consequences of American's Shifting Religious Identities* (New York City: NYU Press, 2014), 62.

24. See Jana Riess, *The Next Mormons: How Millennials are Changing the LDS Church* (New York: Oxford University Press, 2019), 5.

Ostler, commenting on Sherkat's findings, stated, "For this age group, the Church has not been able to attract enough converts to replace those who are leaving with a net overflow of 28%."[25]

Clearly, religion is losing popularity and becoming a curiosity, especially among the younger generation. As more people depart from the faith, the majority of the population will view conservative religion as a threat to society. The moral boundaries established by the commandments of God will increasingly clash with the "you be you" attitude of the day. Some Christian denominations will remain true to their convictions. Others will succumb to social pressure to pacify the people and fill their seats and coffers (see Mormon 8:32–33). "For the time will come when [the people] will not endure sound doctrine; but after their own lusts shall they heap to themselves teachers, having itching ears; And they shall turn away their ears from the truth, and shall be turned unto fables" (2 Timothy 4:3–4). Their churches will "cast away the law of the Lord" (Isaiah 5:24), "justify the wicked for reward" (verse 23), and "call evil good, and good evil" (verse 20).

The more inclusive the world and those churches become, the more exclusive conservative Christianity will seem—and more particularly, The Church of Jesus Christ of Latter-day Saints. Much of the world will increasingly view true Christians as antiquated, bigoted, narrow-minded, judgmental, and hateful. As a result, the world's tolerance for those with Christian convictions will devolve into intolerance. Intolerance will devolve into what society will believe is justified hatred, and they will begin to persecute the followers of Christ (see Matthew 24:9).

The preliminary dividing of the sheep and goats now in progress serves two purposes. One, it causes the sheep to flock together to find support among those with similar convictions. Two, the growing

---

25. David B. Ostler, *Bridges: Ministering to Those Who Question* (Salt Lake City: Greg Kofford Books, 2019), 4.

intolerance for Christian conviction, coupled with the dark nights of the soul they endure, galvanize their faith. When the great tribulation comes and false Christs and false prophets deceive many, the Lord's sheep, His elect, will not be discouraged or deceived because they will have endured other fortifying storms. Instead, they will hear His voice through His prophets and follow Him (see John 10:27).

After the earth's dark night of the soul, it will be cleansed of all iniquity by fire, just as it was once cleansed by flood. Therefore, the earth will have been baptized by water (see 1 Peter 3:18–21) and by fire (see 2 Peter 3:6–7; Doctrine and Covenants 101:24–25). The cleansing fire will not erupt from a natural catastrophe or from man-made missiles, for the Lord will "consume [the wicked] with . . . the brightness of his coming" (2 Thessalonians 2:8). Only the righteous who are worthy to inherit terrestrial or celestial glory will endure the glory of the Lord and remain on the earth during the Millennium.[26] Then the earth will enter the Senior stage of faith, for love will abound in the hearts of all people. Peace will prevail and joy will fill the earth (see Isaiah 2:4; Isaiah 11:6–9; Doctrine and Covenants 101:26).

Key Point Summary

- The stages of faith can be mapped to Kohlberg's stages of moral development.
- The Lord modifies His methods to fit His followers' level of moral development.
- The more we learn to live by correct principles, the more the Lord permits us to govern ourselves.
- We are at the cusp of a universal dark night.

---

26. See *Gospel Principles* (2009), chapter 45.

SUMMARY

"In every crisis there is a message. Crises are nature's way of forcing change—breaking down old structures, shaking loose negative habits so that something new and better can take their place."

—Susan L. Taylor[1]

The dark night of the soul is divinely designed for each of us who experience it. It is a spiritual chrysalis intended to transform us into all the Lord needs us to become and all that we want to become—the best version of us.

Not all experience the dark night. Some experience a singular severe dark night, and others experience many dark nights throughout their lives. Though every spiritual journey is similar, every spiritual journey is different. Each is guided by loving heavenly parents.

The doubts we experience in crises of faith should not be considered the absence of faith but rather the evidence of faith. Faith and doubt are two sides of the same coin. One cannot demonstrate faith

---

1. Susan L. Taylor, "In every crisis," AZ Quotes, accessed Nov. 9, 2022, https://www.azquotes.com/quote/572227.

without doubt; therefore, we should not feel shame or guilt when we doubt. We should simply act in faith despite our doubts because confirmation comes *after* the trial of our faith (see Ether 12:6).

The stages of faith (Child, Adolescent, Young Adult, Adult, and Senior) transform us over a lifetime as we seek to become less self-serving and more serving, increase in love for self and others, suppress pride and grow in humility, become more submissive and meek, and learn to serve with "an eye single to the glory of God" (Doctrine and Covenants 4:5). Some transition through all of the stages of faith in their lifetime and experience the crises of faith at the transition point that proceeds each stage. Others live out their whole lives in an earlier stage and enjoy a fulfilling relationship with their Father in Heaven and Savior and receive all the rewards of eternal life. We should recognize when we have become stagnant at a stage and acknowledge that a crisis of faith at that stage is not God's abandonment of us. It is quite the opposite! It is His firm, gentle call for us to transition to the next stage of faith.

Each endured crisis of faith galvanizes and prepares us for the coming universal dark night. The minor battles we win through each crisis harden and equip us for the coming battle that will deceive all but the very elect (see Matthew 24:24).

As we develop an understanding of the stages of faith and endure our own crises of faith, we are called to mentor others. We should reach out to them and listen with kindness, love, empathy, and acceptance. We should help them understand the stages of faith and equip them with the mindset, tool set, and skill set to endure their periodic winters of faith and the dark night of the soul.

May we learn to rejoice in the Refiner's purifying "furnace of affliction" (Isaiah 48:10) until all of us can see His image in our countenance (see Alma 5:14).

NOTES

NOTES

NOTES

NOTES

About the Author

Rico Maranto grew up in the Bible Belt. He was the only member of The Church of Jesus Christ of Latter-day Saints in his Southern Baptist private school where he found his faith was frequently challenged. He later served as a missionary in Kentucky where he met Bible scholars at nearly every door who could quote scripture to support their criticisms of his sacredly held beliefs. Those experiences fortified him and encouraged him to gain a deeper understanding and testimony of the restored gospel of Jesus Christ.

After his mission, he served in various Church leadership positions. After serving as a bishop for the second time, he suffered a severe and devastating crisis of faith. After enduring his crisis of faith, he desired to support others in crisis.

Rico is a leadership development consultant. He was a contributing author for *Servant Leadership in Action* by Ken Blanchard and Renee Broadwell and authored two magazine articles and two children's books. He has an MS in organizational leadership and human resources management and resides in Kingwood, TX, with his wife, Elizabeth, and their four children.

Scan to visit

www.ricomaranto.com

235